Growth Hacking

Techniques, Disruptive Technology -
How 40 Companies Made It BIG –
Online Growth Hacker Marketing
Strategy.

Robert Peters

Foreword

Writing a book about growth hacking can be a little like the proverbial hopeless task of nailing Jell-O to the wall. At just the point that you think you have control of the thing, it shimmies out of your grasp.

The term "growth hacking" has only been around since 2010 and is credited to an article by Sean Ellis on the blog Startup Marketing (startup-marketing.com) entitled, "Find a Growth Hacker for Your Startup."

Ellis begins the post by saying, "Once startups are ready to scale, their biggest challenge is often hiring someone capable of leading the growth charge. A marketer with the right talents and approach can kick some serious ass once product-market fit and an efficient conversion / monetization process have been proven."

A few paragraphs later, he defines the term "growth hacker" in this way, "A growth hacker is a person whose true north is growth. Everything they do is scrutinized by its potential impact on scalable growth. Is positioning important? Only if a case can be made that it is important for driving sustainable growth (FWIW [for what it's worth], a case can generally be made)."

Since Ellis' post, many writers and industry pundits have run with the term "growth hacker" and made it as magically elusive and sometimes as questionably valid as the Reagan era "voodoo economics." Here's how I see growth hacking . . . and you don't need a cauldron and a spell book to make it work.

Growth hacking is marketing for the 21st century.

"Really?" you say, "That's all you've got for me?"

Go watch a few episodes of the television series *Mad Men* and come back and tell me if a 1960s era ad campaign would work today.

When I first began working online in the early 1990s doing web design, animated GIFs were all the rage. I think now about the pulsating rule bars and spinning globes that were the "in" thing and cringe. It's as bad as 1960s era fashion, clouds of cigarette smoke, and lava lamps.

Okay, lava lamps are still cool, but I digress.

In the first chapter of this book, I try to introduce you to the figure of a growth hacker and invite you into his mindset. As you read through the text, including the profiles of 40 companies that have successfully used growth hacking techniques, you'll come to understand the importance of that one fundamental quality *a growth mindset*.

The growth hackers at the companies I discuss expected their efforts to grow from day one, they wanted that growth, and they focused all their efforts on achieving growth.

- Elliot Schmukler at LinkedIn analyzed the channels that brought users to the site and brilliantly linked the actions of "actives" to "inactives" to grow membership.

- Ride-for-hire company Uber cultivated a local market roll out plan and refined and repeated it one market at a time.

- Etsy exploited an overlooked group of sellers that eBay was pushing out and catered specifically to their needs.

- Pinterest built interest and desire with an invitation-only beta and seeded the site with professional content from designers who immediately grasped the concept of building online inspiration boards.

- Yelp leveraged the desire for first-person recommendations with perceived authority, all built on the founder's need for a doctor when he came down with a flu.

- Square founder Jim McKelvey lost a $2,000 sale on a piece of art glass at a fair because he couldn't accept a credit card, so he founded a company that brought mobile payment technology to cell phones and tablets regardless of location.

These examples are only samples of the strategies employed by some of the most successful growth hackers of our time who understand that the first principle of growth hacking is that markets *change* and successful marketers change with them.

In fact, everything about web access and use has changed and is continuing to do so around us, thanks to the rise of the smartphone and the connected tablet. Mobile devices are generating more and more web consumption, including watching streaming video content. Growing your business in this climate demands meeting the needs of the mobile user.

The more the cellphone providers can pump out in terms of affordable mobile bandwidth and the more free wifi spots become available in municipalities, the more that trend won't just grow, but explode exponentially.

The days of sitting down in front of a desktop computer to do something online are rapidly passing into the dim recesses of memory. People want to be able to buy things from their phones, hail a ride, meet people, video conference – be *connected*.

Old marketing concepts don't work in a world that is online to that extent. I used to have a running argument with a friend who insisted to me that the Internet is not a "place." I still beg to differ that it is indeed a place, and the portals of entry are now no farther away than our mobile devices.

If your particular branded portal, be it an app or a website, that leads to your product or service is not optimized for the mobile user experience, you're in trouble. All the beautiful SEO in the world won't save you.

Growth hacking isn't about running "an ad campaign," it's about *living* a constant philosophy of growth – never resting on your laurels, being prepared to change your course with the needs of the marketplace. In short, growth hacking is as dynamic as the Internet itself.

And there's no ONE way to do it. That's where the nailing Jell-O part comes in. A lot of people are saying they can teach growth hacking, but I think the age old model of the master and the apprentice is much more applicable.

There really is something of the Jedi knight in the successful growth hacker. You can learn all kinds of techniques from stories about growth hacks that worked. The bulk of this text is about doing that very thing, profiling companies and their growth hacks and absorbing the lessons they have to teach those who come after them.
But to really be "one with the Force?" That's between you and your product, your market, your customers and users, your software engineers – and likely your financier. Growth hacking is about finding the sweet spot where inspiration and perspiration meet.

It's about using the most up-to-date tools to analyze market trends and then rolling the bones to make them work. It's about calculated decisions and out and out scrappy trickery.

When it works, it's a thing of beauty and not surprisingly, there are already legendary growth hacking stories like

AirBnB's bot-driven hack of Craigslist in the absence of a publicly available API.

Not all growth hacks fall into such maverick territory, but they do show that there's still something of a frontier element to the online world and still plenty of opportunity for innovative start-ups to enter the fray and make it big.

Exclusive Free Offer

Join other Growth Hackers who want to discover more resources, techniques, methods and free videos on growth hacks in our unique **FREE** club – Exclusive to owners of this book.

See page 23 on how to join easily in seconds (and free)

Table of Contents

Table of Contents

Table of Contents

Chapter 1 - Meet the Growth Hacker

The question I encounter more than any other with people who are new to this topic isn't, "How do I growth hack?" A surprising number of people are still at, "What the heck *is* growth hacking?"

Since growth hacking is as much an art as a skill, you're right to ask both questions in the beginning of your understanding of this exciting new approach to marketing.

A "growth hacker" is a hybrid beast, a skilled mix of a technical genius and a marketer. He's leading the way in the rapid development of a new "standard" business model. In the process, he's making every definition of "marketing" you ever learned completely irrelevant.

The Growth Hacking Mindset

At the very least, growth hackers are rewriting the standard "best practices" of marketing. Many are doing so from the coding perspective of the genius geeks who built the Internet as we know it today.

Growth hackers don't see marketing as an activity, per se, but a fundamental aspect of how a product or service is designed and built. Subsequent versions or iterations are optimized and shared on the basis of ongoing evaluations of success.

These evaluations and adjustments are assumed to be infinite and are repeated multiple times. The major goal is massive and rapid growth, not being wedded to any one design or operational model.

In this mindset everything becomes fair game for the critical eye of the growth hacker. They don't so much ask, "How well is our marketing email written?" as "How *deliverable* is our email?"

Marketing language is not as important as the mechanism that sends the email and encourages the message it contains to be passed on from one user to the next.

A growth hacker won't be satisfied with an attractive or well-laid out website, he'll ask why the site doesn't load 2 seconds faster and why the Facebook opt-in link isn't more prominently placed.

Such factors are no longer issues for the technical or design team, but for the growth hacker charged with winning the market. His end goal is always a self-perpetuating machine that is so well oiled, it constantly grows itself.

Armed with the ability to track, test, and improve every imaginable Internet metric, growth hackers are not attracted to the enormous gambles that were once the lifeblood of the dot come world.

They don't do anything that is unnecessary or counterproductive, and they know the value of small, but highly elegant strategies.

Lessons Learned from Hotmail and Gmail

Take, for instance, the example of Hotmail, a classic in every growth hacking conversation. The simple strategy there was the answer to the question, "Can we put a message at the bottom of everyone's screen who gets an email from our service?"

That translated to an advertisement for the product on every email sent. In six months, Hotmail had 1 million members, a figure the service then doubled in just five weeks. When Microsoft bought Hotmail in December 1997 for $400 million, there were nearly 10 million users.

Hotmail took exactly 30 months to acquire 30 million users! The initial investment in the service was $300,000. Most everyone I know would be happy with a profit margin of $399,700,000!

When Google launched Gmail the company followed many of the same growth strategies. They built an excellent product, but created curiosity and buzz by making its initial use by invitation only.

The number of potential invites was increased along with the existing user base, spreading Gmail usage and popularity from person to person. Now, Gmail is the dominant and best free email service with 425 million users reported in 2012.

Growth is the Focus

Growth hackers are charged with taking "nothing" and turning it into "something" as fast as they possibly can.

To do so, the traditional marketing playbook goes out the window in favor of all things trackable, testable, and scalable.

Once upon a time the buzz words of the business world were publicity, advertising, branding, and "mind share." All growth hackers do is pursue *growth*.

Their tools are things like email, pay-per-click, blogs, and platform APIs. Their mantra is almost Biblical, "And users beget users, who beget users, who beget . . . "

Fill a Need, No Matter What

The basic principle of marketing still applies, "Who are my customers and where are they?" In classic marketing, the strategy used to reach those customers was honed and refined, but the business and product remained basically the same.

Growth hackers believe changing the entire business model is completely fair game. They're not interested in just re-designing the cereal box, nor are they even dedicated to making the cereal! The only goal is to generate explosive reactions and complete loyalty from the customer.

The best marketing decision is to fulfill a real and compelling need for those customers. If that means changing the business itself to reach them, the growth hacker says, "Let's do it!"

He is a relentless follower of the Socratic Method. Question every assumption repeatedly and beware complacency.

- Who is this product for?
- Why would someone use this product?
- Why do *I* use this product?
- Is this the right product for the job?
- Is this the right job for the product?

And on and on and on until you get the Holy Grail — Product Market Fit (PMF).

Match Making with Early Adopters

Matching the way products are marketed with the way prospects learn about and shop for those products is a crucial aspect of growth hacking.

Early adopters are key to this process and can make or break a business launch. Any product or service that can, in the beginning, grab and keep the interest of early adopters that become loyal and fanatical users stands a much greater chance of achieving the kind of explosive growth that is the ultimate goal.

If you're launching a product or service and you don't know where to find those early adopters? You don't know your industry or service sector well enough to even think about launching!

It Takes a Tribe

Building that army of passionate, loyal users is today's version of branding. If you have that army, what some growth hackers call your "tribe," you don't have to worry so much about how you maintain your pre-existing brand as it relates to a specific product or service. Your tribe will be receptive to whatever you offer.

This is a lesson that self-published authors are learning. The new product model in self-publishing is the serial novel offered after the fashion of a television series. This type of fiction is shorter, and appears on a regular schedule.

Fans are passionately loyalty to the characters and the world they inhabit, so they are hungry for each new book. As additional readers discover the books, they are equally hungry for all the titles in the existing catalog. Sales for older titles are generated at the same time that the desire for new titles is amplified.

Some self-published authors have fewer than 1,000 loyal readers, but they are earning six-figure incomes, completely redefining the concept of what it means to be a "bestselling" author.

Not all of these books are great works of literature. In fact, most of them aren't. That's not the point. The books sell, and they generate excellent long-term income for the authors. Is it any wonder that traditional publishers fear the growing power of independent authors and the rise of the ebook?

Every start-up, even if it's a self-published zombie novel, is designed to be one thing — a growth engine.

Going Viral Isn't an Accident

Most people think "going viral" is an accident, and if you've shot a YouTube video that has generated buzz, it probably is. If you're a growth hacker, however, you don't view going viral or achieving "virality" as something that happens after the fact.

You know that successful products are inherently worth sharing and you facilitate and encourage that sharing every way you possibly can. You know that products and services have to advertise themselves, and you know the value of "behavioral residue." Social currency is free, but it is also invaluable to the point of being priceless.

Virality isn't an accident. It should be hardwired into your product or service. You don't just want a new customer, you want a lifelong user who will happily turn right around and market your product for you like a religious witness.

Investing in strategies that improve sales and marketing is no longer the goal. Creating fanatically happy users is the be all and end all of the growth hacker's day.

Investing in refining and improving the product or the service to retain and optimize customer loyalty is everything — even if it's a 2 second faster load time on a website! Ridiculous, you say?

- A 5% increase in customer retention rates translate to a 30% increase in profitability according to Bain & Company.

- The chance of selling to a new prospect is 5-20% — to an existing customer, 60-70%.

Growth hackers achieve success by doing whatever they have to do not just to bring customers into the "funnel," but into the "family." Budgets go toward targeted product and service refinement or even redirection, not advertising.

In this model, the price of being "wrong" is greatly reduced because you grant yourself the freedom to change on the fly. As long as your customers are happy and using your service or buying your product, you are a success.

How Do I Learn to be a Growth Hacker?

As I said earlier, growth hacking is as much an art as a science. The tools to grow one product or service won't necessarily work for another. This is not a set process of steps, or a "do this" and then "do that" way of thinking.

In my opinion, one of the best ways to become a growth hacker is to study at the feet of masters. To that end, I'm devoting the remainder of this book to profiling some of the most impressive (if not always the best known) examples of how products and services have benefited from innovative growth hacking techniques.

"But wait," you say. "If I've never heard of a company or a service, how can it be a success?" Because each of these entities has a dedicated set of core users. Growth hacking even redesigns what it means to be a success!

Remember those self-published authors? Many are remodeling their homes and funding their children's college education on the reading tastes of fewer than 1,000 dedicated readers.

To a Stephen King, a readership that small might not be a success, but to an indie author, it's their ticket to a completely changed lifestyle. Both authors are "successes," but their success is defined differently.

Stephen King is an internationally recognized author. The indie guy? His mortgage is paid off and his kid is going to college. That's more than enough success in his book.

As you begin to read the profiles that comprise the bulk of this book, take your first step toward becoming a growth hacker by throwing out both the rulebook *and* the dictionary.

You truly are about to enter a "brave new world," and frankly, it's a pretty exciting landscape out there!

Exclusive FREE Offer – How to Join

Join other Growth Hackers in our unique **FREE** club –
Exclusive to owners of this book (and receive **free updates**
to this book in the future)

It's quick and easy to sign up. As we release more case
studies, discover new hacks, more methods that are really
working we'll let you know. You can receive discounts on
tortoise food, supplies and more including connecting with
other owners. Here's how in 2 simple steps…

Step 1

Go to http://www.GrowthHacking.me

Enter your name and email address and click "Join"

Step 2

Confirm your subscription. As soon as you sign up we'll
send you an email asking you to confirm the details are
correct. Just click the link in the email and you'll be joined
free.

If you don't receive the email, please check your spam
folder and that you used the correct email address.

It's as easy as that. Any questions please email
growthhacking@bleppublishing.com and where possible
we will help.

LinkedIn

LinkedIn is a social networking site for business professionals that was founded in 2002 and launched in 2003. In 2008, there were about 13 million users before growth hacking strategies employed by Elliot Schmukler caused the California-based platform to explode. Currently, LinkedIn has 259 million members in 200 countries speaking 20 languages.

The value propositions of the LinkedIn idea were clear from the beginning. The service sought to make business networking easier by enhancing communication among colleagues, and facilitating valuable introductions thus broadening connections.

Recruiters, job hunters, and reporters immediately saw the potential in LinkedIn's information repository, but about 50% of the users were passive. They created profiles initially, but then did little with them, which significantly slowed growth.

In an attempt to remedy this situation, Schmukler first worked to understand all the ways in which new users organically discovered LinkedIn. Primarily, this occurred through email invitations and search engine queries that directed people to member's profiles and home pages. Both channels worked, but were in need of reinforcement.

Analysis revealed that when emails were sent to users notifying them of a profile view, active users clicked through at a rate of 20%, but inactive members responded with only 5% click though.

Schmukler could have worked on redesigning the emails to maximize effectiveness, or conducted "drip" email campaigns to lure inactives back in, but instead he decided to develop links between actives and inactives through an "endorsement" feature.

The campaign worked, until September 2013 when customers balked, filing a lawsuit against LinkedIn. The plaintiffs claimed the service appropriated their identities for its marketing purposes, tunneling into their email accounts and mining their contacts to broaden the reach of the service's invitations.

At the heart of the complaint is LinkedIn's encouragement for new members to invite others to the network during the sign-up process. Without question, the aggressive emails, whether through invitations or endorsements for existing members, have been a significant growth strategy for LinkedIn.

Other companies, including Facebook, have also received scathing criticism from users for similar strategies that, though effective, can be perceived as compromising the privacy of members' contact lists. Fortunately, by the time the lawsuit was filed, LinkedIn had already established a sufficient user base for growth to take off on its own.

This points to the truism that growth hacking strategies don't have to last forever. A questionable strategy like the one used by LinkedIn can be effective in the short term so that when the company is "caught" and compelled to shift gears, the existing benefits outweigh any negatives of the forced course correction.

Uber

Uber was founded in 2009 as "Ubercab," and launched in June 2010. The service connects passengers with vehicles for hire. Users make reservations via the Uber mobile app. The cost is similar to that of metered taxis, but all money exchanged is handled by Uber, not the drivers.

Like the digital loyalty platform Belly, Uber focused intensely on one launch city at a time, starting in San Francisco where early growth was fueled primarily by word of mouth. Like most successful services, Uber started with a high value solution to a very specific problem.

Hailing or hiring a cab is a nightmare involving delay and cumbersome, old-fashioned cash payments. That is *if* you can find a cab to hail. With Uber, which is integrated with Google maps, users can see the available cars nearest to them, as well as the driver's information and ratings.

Once a car is hired, a meeting point is set and scheduled, with the driver calling or texting to confirm the reservation. The cost of the ride is charged to the user's credit card — no need to deal with cash. The entire process removes the friction from hiring a cab, which is immediately clear to anyone who does so on a regular basis.

Based primarily on ease of use and satisfied early adopters, Uber went from launch in June 2010 to almost 6,000 users / 20,000 rides in six months. By choosing to launch in San Francisco, where cab service is notoriously bad, they not only illustrated their value proposition, but also became known in an important tech community.

To enhance their visibility, the company also sponsored tech events and offered free rides to show the quality of their cars and drivers.

Word of mouth is so critical to Uber's growth that the company says that 95% of all riders have heard about the service from someone who has used it previously. They estimate that for every seven Uber rides, one new Uber user is generated.

Not surprisingly then, referrals are a strong growth engine. Each user receives an assigned referral code. If a new user signs up with the code, both parties are awarded $10 toward their next Uber ride.

Growth is especially strong in some cities where the benefit to riders is even greater. Chicago, for instance, has a major nightlife and sports scene, but intense weather that can make getting around extremely difficult. In Washington, D.C., the service has seen month-over-month growth of 30-40%.

The Uber growth engine is so effective, the company simply repeats it over and over again:

- Intense launches in well-chosen cities where a real need exists.

- Caveats like free rides to gain media and potential user attention.

- The "wow" experience of using the app for the first time and having a frictionless car-for-hire experience.

- Word of mouth from satisfied and enthusiastic customers.

Their steady success has given Uber the necessary confidence to trust the value of the service it offers. This is not a tentative company. They believe that once a user has the Uber experience, they will prefer the service over using a cab.

That confidence allows the company to routinely hand out $20 ride credits to new users, an incentive that removes any remaining barriers for new riders to become long-term customers.

By October 2013 on the strength of these successes, Uber raised more than $307 million in investment capital.

Etsy

In 2005, the popular online marketplace Etsy launched in Brooklyn. Through the service, small sellers offer handmade goods and vintage items that are at least 20 years old.

Though the design of the site is slick and appealing, the tone is "crafty" with the feel of an upscale flea market or art fair that works brilliantly. In August 2013, the company reported a user base of 30 million, with 1 million sellers, and more than $1 billion in recorded transactions.

The Etsy CEO, Chad Dickerson, insisted that the company focus on both product and corporate culture. His goal was to create a more authentic and personalized e-commerce experience.

As major competitor EBay moved farther away from support for small sellers, Etsy stepped in to fill the void. The market for handmade goods might be relatively limited, but it is also a thriving and popular one.

The corporate culture at Etsy evolved with the small seller in mind, providing favorable economics to the artisans it hoped to attract as users. On Etsy, sellers are charged 3.5% per sale, plus listing fees. On eBay, they pay 9% plus listing fees.

Also, Etsy uses a fixed price model rather than auctions, which gives artists a better chance of actually recouping the worth of their product. An ongoing frustration for eBay sellers who work with auctions are items that sell for low dollar amounts with free shipping offers. In these situations, the seller often loses money on the product.

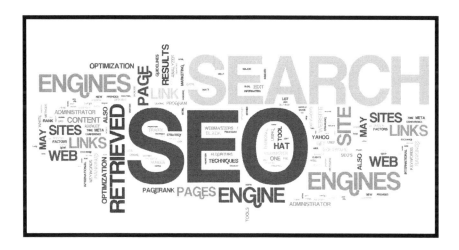

In 2011, Etsy sellers moved $525 million in goods sold. By 2012, however, the marketplace grew 71% for $895.1 million in transactions. At the same time, more than 10 million new members signed on, boosting total membership to 22 million.

Etsy wisely offered more than just lower fees to sellers, who were also given access to educational materials to become savvy in creating good SEO for their shops and for promoting themselves on social media.

In 2012, Etsy launched a mobile app for both Android and the Apple iOS, which boosted the site's market reach and increased user engagement and impulse buys.

The seller culture is highly personal. Each user has an inbox and sales include personal conversations that might be a simple thank you, or questions regarding customization of an order, like ring sizing or similar details.

The growth hacking "walk-aways" from Etsy are incredibly simple, but also incredibly effective.

- The company has excellent leadership that looked to culture and product over quarterly profits.

- The leadership identified and catered to an important cultural zeitgeist. Buyers wanted authentic commerce purchases in a true marketplace atmosphere.

While smaller than eBay or Amazon, Etsy focused on meeting the needs of its target audience. Consequently, eBay sees only about 18 percent annual growth and Amazon tallies about 34%.

Upstart Etsy with its crafty feel and marketplace culture has an annual growth rate of around 70% in an arguably small, but certainly booming niche.

Pinterest

Pinterest is a visual discovery tool that allows users to create and share collections of bookmarks they've assembled as boards, which can be followed as a whole, or "re-pinned" in part.

The concept as it is now understood is incredibly simple and oddly addictive, but when Pinterest launched in 2010, the first users, attracted by an invite-only beta, weren't quite sure what to do with it.

The first crop of users thought they were looking at some alternate version of Instagram and floundered until a smart growth strategy led to the creation of an insta-following hack. Rather than have to seek out boards to follow, new users automatically found themselves subscribed to the most popular feeds on the site.

This was an excellent move on the part of Pinterest designers since the initial pin content on the site was quite high — and remains so today. Many of the first invites went to professionals in the areas of art, design, architecture, fashion, and crafts who immediately understood the concept of "inspiration boards."

Those fist design savvy users set the tone and showed subsequent Pinterest members how to use their boards to create their own collections with no regard to "rules." A board can be anything a user wants to make of it. Pinterest is about the curation and sharing of inspirational ideas.

This spirit leads to an unusually high level of subsequent sharing on Twitter and Facebook. The average Pinterest user seems to want to say, "Hey, look at what I found!" This generates high social engagement and fuels new user sign ups.

Consequently, Pinterest users become quite passionate about curating the content of their boards. Many are also participants in online gatherings like conventions and fairs where they broaden the site's user base through enthusiastic word of mouth.

It's common for boards to be linked to blogs and websites. A collection on Pinterest is easier to build and update than a web page and has a higher chance of generating user involvement. The visual presentation of the boards is clean and compelling.

Once users are signed up, they automatically receive a subscription to weekly updates of activity on boards they follow that include thumbnail images of the most recent pins. They can also search for and follow users among their Facebook fans.

This aggressive policy of notification enhances the already highly social climate and has steadily driven user adoption. Consequently, Pinterest posts some impressive numbers.

From launch to July 2013, the site gained 70 million users and has about 2.5 million page views per month.

Thanks to well-designed apps that preserve the Pinterest experience, 75% of daily traffic is from mobile sources.

Approximately 5 million items per day are pinned.

As of October 2013, the company had a valuation of $3.8 billion, even though it has no set monetization strategy and technically makes nothing. (The company has, however, raised more than $563 million in investment capital.)

Yelp

Yelp, Inc., which is now a San Francisco-based multinational, was founded in 2004 by Jeremy Stoppelman and Russel Simmons. The idea began when Stoppelman came down with the flu and needed a recommendation for a doctor, but couldn't get one.

The experience gave him an idea for a website where people could ask for local recommendations of any kind via email rather than relying exclusively on their personal connections. On Yelp, users would always "know" someone even if they were new to an area and didn't yet have an established network.

The idea of user submitted reviews for venues and services wasn't new, but the Yelp founders early on turned their focus to social engagement to grow their user base. Reviewers filled out profiles, friended one another, and exchanged accolades for their reviews.

Rather than relying on anonymous opinions, Yelp users built reputations for themselves and began to construct well thought out and in-depth reviews unlike those seen on other sites in order to preserve those reputations.

So-called "super" users were classed as the Yelp Elite, and were invited to parties and special events, which only helped to incentivize more prolific and positive behavior within the Yelp community.

By 2006, the company's growth campaign included stickers in store windows. With just this level of engagement, the site garnered 15 million visitors per month by 2008, but then Yelp launched an iPhone app with integration for business owners to manage their own listings.

API integration and apps became Yelp's primary focus so that sharing information and reviews along with user rewards could occur spontaneously and in any location at any time. The company also hired community managers for its major markets.

Yelp's rapid growth and popularity hinged on its local approach that put users first while offering them a service they really wanted. That, coupled with honest reviews created a highly appealing perception of accuracy and trust.

By then integrating business owners themselves into the community, Yelp gave small local entrepreneurs a chance to plug into free, goodwill-based advertising through reviews as well as by purchasing ads and offering coupons and daily deals.

Without question the proliferation of smartphones aided Yelp's growth, like that of many other sites with social components. Well-engineered apps foster social engagement through immediacy, and have proven to be powerful growth hacking tools.

By November 2012, Yelp reported that 45% of the traffic to its site originated from mobile devices, with approximately 1.4 million mobile users signed up by June 2013.

Over the past ten years, Yelp has proven to be flexible in its approach to features, enhancing tools like apps that have worked well for them, while quietly de-emphasizing options like daily deals that proved too competitive with other site features.

This willingness to tailor the user experience remains one of Yelp's greatest strengths and keeps its community strong and vital.

Square

San Francisco-based Square is a mobile payments and merchant services aggregator. It allows individuals and businesses in the U.S., Canada, and Japan to accept debit and credit cards on iOS and Android smartphones and tablets.

The cardholder's information can be captured either by swiping the cards through an attachment that connects to the earphone jack of the device or by manually entering the data. The company was founded in 2009 and launched its first app the following year.

Perhaps nothing has done more to drive the growth of Square than the fact that it fills a real need in a simple and elegant way. The company has completely reimagined how small businesses accept payments.

Before Square appeared on the scene, only registered merchants could accept credit card payments, which was an expensive and difficult process. It required a complicated application and the acquisition of specialized equipment.

In addition, the fee structure associated with different types of transactions often made accepting cards too expensive or forced merchants to set minimum purchase limits that customers found off putting.

The idea for Square was born of a personal experience by the company's co-founder, Jim McKelvey. He was unable to sell a $2,000 piece of glass at an art fair because he couldn't accept a credit card. McKelvey immediately saw the need for a new solution for merchants to accept payments in all kinds of venues.

Square's growth was certainly not hampered in any way by the high profile of McKelvey's partner, Jack Dorsey, co-founder of Twitter. Not only did Dorsey bring personal influence to the Square project, he aggressively sought early customers and investors with an audaciously entitled list of, "140 Reasons Why Square Will Fail."

Each time Dorsey put the list in front of potential investors, he neatly offered a counterpoint for every objection raised. That piqued the interest of investors, cultivated a "can do" reputation for Square as a company, and gained a lot of attention in the tech press.

Coupled with product demonstrations that highlighted the integrated hardware / software solution's ease of use, the "in your face" approach immediately communicated Square's high value propositions.

Setup and configuration of the point of sales systems was only the beginning, however. Once in place, Square offered participating merchants insights mined from the collected data and delivered the material via a gorgeous reporting package.

For instance, Square can pinpoint the most popular menu items for restaurant owners and target their busiest days of the week and month. Small businesses can then implement big business strategies that enhance customer loyalty and satisfaction — all while reducing the friction in purchases. With Square, they could make intelligent "big" business decisions for a fraction of the price those metrics would otherwise cost.

The growth team at Square could have stopped there and likely still have had a winning product, but they insisted that the hardware (the plug-in reader), be as eye-catching as possible. Paying for an item through the Square system always generates conversation.

"What is that thing?" customers ask, as they experience signing with their fingers on an iPad or iPhone and promptly receiving their receipt via email. Simply put, Square makes it fun to pay by credit card, and that generates word of mouth. Consumers like novel experiences, and they like to be surprised.

Early on, Square established a close relationship with Apple, which stocked and sold the readers for $10 in every store after the company launched, and made the app available for download in the iTunes store. When Square then received a strategic investment from Visa, it gained a boost in perceived credibility that led to even higher rates of adoption.

All of these elements combined to create a passionate user base. Square customers are more than willing to rave about the product, which only generates more growth. When a user pays for an item for the first time on Square it is almost impossible not to tell the "story."

Square's success at developing its product and growing its user base is a perfect example of filling a real need with a beautifully designed solution that is the focus of consistent improvement all targeted toward enhancing the user experience.

Square's valuation has jumped from $45 million in December 2009 to $5 billion in January 2014, with no slowing of its growth and ongoing merchant adoption in sight.

Belly

Belly is a digital loyalty platform launched in 2011. Customers earn points or redeem rewards at participating stores by using a physical "Bellycard" or a mobile app. An in-store tablet serves as the establishment's Belly "hub" and is the user point of access.

The exchange of data allows businesses to establish email communication with their customers, gain better exposure on social media sites, and collect information on which they can base better business decisions to create relationships and increase customer loyalty.

After a pre-determined number of check-ins, loyal users are automatically prompted to review the store on Yelp, which further enhances word of mouth. This slick, fun, and frictionless system was developed by the Belly growth team through a graduated system of highly localized roll outs.

This old-fashioned "boots on the ground" approach began in Chicago where the team interviewed hundreds of merchants to better understand their needs and the unique obstacles they faced in their area.

The research paid off by helping the team to understand that merchants wanted an easy, affordable way to build long-term, deep relationships with customers that offered measurable returns.

The developers at Belly then set about building a focused solution for customer relationship management and retention. Their target audience, small and medium businesses, is a notoriously difficult market sector.

SMBs are slow to accept new technologies and have limited funds, making them the very definition of "hard sell." Belly overcame this skepticism with a clearly articulated value proposition and a very low-friction adoption process. The company's all-in-one plans start at $79 a month and included all the necessary hardware.

After leveraging local customer development in Chicago and learning more about SMBs in the process, Belly launched in Austin, Texas at the annual South By Southwest tech conference, thus gaining both a second market and the attention of influential trendsetters.

Smart rollouts in carefully targeted markets became Belly's repeat strategy, which, along with the continued development of the Belly app, spread word of mouth awareness.

Not only is the Belly app integrated with Facebook for easy sharing, but the reward system has a "gamified" approach customers find appealing.

The growth hackers at Belly have designed a system that hits four levels of psychological rewards for users:

- the rush of discovering something new
- competitive satisfaction of earning points
- development of perceived status in the system
- monetary benefits

Each of these elements is a powerful driver for sharing and adoption, especially among groups of friends where the competitive element of Belly use easily takes hold.

As soon as consumers start asking businesses if they are members of the Belly network, the owners get interested, fearing they might be missing out on an important sales driver. This curiosity leverages growth in business memberships as a by-product of customer use, thus making Belly more self-sustaining as it grows.

The strategy has taken Belly from 17,000 users and 275 member merchants in December 2011 to a presence in 6,000 businesses spread over 46 states with more than two million users in July 2013.

This includes strategic partnerships with national retail chains like Chik-Fil-A and Dairy Queen, and more recently, full integration with Apple's Passbook and Google Wallet.

Evernote

Evernote offers a suite of software and services that are designed to allow note taking and archiving across a wide range of devices and operating systems. The company launched its closed beta in 2008 and gained 1 million users in 446 days.

(The closed beta alone drew 250,000 in four months capitalizing on the sense of exclusivity such invitations carry.)

From there the growth curve grew steadily shorter:

- 222 days to reach 2 million
- 133 days to reach 3 million
- 108 days to reach 4 million
- 83 days to reach 5 million
- 52 days to reach 6 million

It is now estimated that just under 20,000 new users sign up for Evernote daily.

The developers at Evernote have, since the beginning, focused on the user experience, but in all honesty, the company benefited enormously from timing. They came along just as smartphones were taking off and quality, useful apps were in exceptionally high demand.

They had their first app out of beta and ready for the launch of the iPhone App Store in June 2008. As more app stores followed, they proved to be high-quality distribution channels for Evernote.

Regardless of the device or operating system, Evernote was there when the store opened for business, prominently featured and ready for download. This is a policy Evernote continues to follow. They already have an app for the much hyped Google Glass wearable computer.

Timing was not the only component of Evernote's success, however. Their designers have created an impressive cross-platform experience with no file size limitations and no complex rules. Regardless of the device or operating system, all platforms sync up seamlessly.

Evernote is totally customizable, allowing users to organize and archive their data into what the company calls their "second brain." The value proposition is so clear and so simple that early in the company's existence, a dedicated user in Switzerland floated Evernote a $500,000 loan based purely on his own passionate use of the product.

These are the kinds of users that can become Evernote Ambassadors, representing the company at meet ups and events where they demonstrate how they use the product and hand out premium trial coupons.

Clearly the word of mouth for the service is excellent. Evernote puts so much emphasis on product superiority, they spend nothing on user acquisition through traditional channels like SEO (search engine optimization) or SEM (search engine marketing).

Finally, Evernote works on a "freemium" model. Users receive access to free, basic service at sign up with an option to upgrade, with more features and storage space. This gets people in the door and in a position to become invested. The longer someone uses Evernote, the more likely they are to pay for the service.

The company also employs a referral program. New users who sign up on referral get a month of the premium service, while the referring member earns points toward various perks like more space, gift cards, or even lunch with the teach at headquarters.

Most recently Evernote has begun to develop product extensions like Evernote Hello for contact management, Evernote clearly for distraction free reading and writing, and even an Evernote Moleskine notebook (each page can be photographed and uploaded to the user's account.)

By keeping the emphasis on the user experience, Evernote built an exceptionally loyal user community. Certainly the company benefited from superior timing, but they have also engineered and consistently improved a cross platform application with true long-term functionality.

Hubspot

Hubspot was founded in spring 2006 during a New Enterprise class on the MIT campus. It is a software platform for inbound marketing that helps companies attract visitors, convert leads, and close on sales/deals.

Users can manage all of their web content and social media accounts in one location, with tools in place to measure success rates by leads and customers. This is a more effective use of collected data than the traditional analytics of page views, time on page, and bounce rate among others.

Hubspot began with 3 customers in 2006 and by 2013 had 10,595.

The company follows a strategy of offering daily free content including its popular website grader, which analyzed more than 2 million websites in its first three years of operation.

The HubSpot philosophy is that free content brings people to the company's site thus generating quality leads at a lesser cost than could be achieved with traditional marketing techniques.

The website grader and the HubSpot blog generate the most traffic, with instructional and promotional webinars driving conversions. (Each blog post ends with an "opt in" for HubSpot webinars.) The company credits these three channels with 75% of its lead generation.

Some webinars are more successful than others. In January 2011, for instance, a webinar on the science of Facebook drew in 13,000 attendees.

This overall strategy is referred to as "inbound marketing," which the HubSpot team thinks of as building and owning the sources of your lead generation.

Outbound marketing, according to this line of thinking, puts companies in the same position as "renters," depending on platforms owned by others to build traffic.

The company claims that inbound leads converts twice as often as outbound leads because they are of a higher quality in the first place. This is the continued justification for the emphasis on free content creation that caters to the point of view of the potential customer.

GitHub

GitHub, a web-based software development environment, launched in 2008, initially focused on facilitating projects that used the Git system for revision control.

The idea for the site was developed on a whim over a weekend. In 3 years and 8 months, however, it grew to become a site with a million code repositories. In December 2013, that number reached a staggering 10 million.

At its core, GitHub is a success because it solves a problem. The Git version-control system developed by Linus Torvalds in 2005 made collaboration possible for Linux kernel development, but it was far from an "easy" solution.

Prior to GitHub, developers who wanted to contribute code to an open source project were forced to download the source code, create their changes locally, and compile a list of those changes called a patch. This would then be emailed to the project's maintainer for approval or rejection.

On GitHub, developers can "fork" or copy any code repository that has been made public and modify it within their own account. They then share the changes with the repository's owner with a "pull request." If the owner likes the changes, they're merged into the original repository.

All of the friction that was once standard to software collaboration is removed with a solution that is manageable, seamless, and completely scalable.

GitHub customers can have free access, but if they subscribe to a private account, they have more freedom to leverage GitHub's resources within their development teams.

Some of the biggest GitHub customers include The White House, Facebook, Twitter, LinkedIn, and Amazon.

GitHub has grown so quickly because it is inherently driven by network dynamics. The larger the overall code repository grows, the more attractive the site is to developers.

There are social networking functions built in to the site including feeds and tools to follow users. Live conversations and chats are central to the GitHub culture, which also includes wikis of constantly edited and updated information.

In just six years, GitHub has become the most important social network for computer engineers and an invaluable repository for code elements. New users are drawn to the community by many channels, including invites from existing members as well as through open source collaborative efforts.

The site has become a channel for technical marketers and professionals to reach developers, and repositories of code are often used by members as resumes of their work.

The free public beta of GitHub switched to a freemium model by user request. People wanted private repositories, and they were willing to pay for them. The cost is still remarkably low, $7 for individuals and $25 for organizations, but at the enterprise tier, the company can earn millions per year.

Although GitHub obviously came hardwired with a formula for success due to the unique niche it fills, the company has smartly embraced a collaborative corporate culture that attracts and keeps good minds. Employees can work any time they like, from anywhere, and on anything that attracts their interest.

There are no managers and no delegated tasks. Employees hold themselves accountable and are driven by their passion for the work they do. The GitHub philosophy is that truly committed and engaged people will always return superior quality work because they are doing what they love. This is a very high-level expression of the growth hacking concept of market fit.

There is no reticence at GitHub to beta test new functionality. Bugs are uncovered in real time, problems fixed on the fly, and hidden potential uncovered. It is something of a free-for-all atmosphere that clearly works.

The "product," in this case a productive and social collaborative environment, has a high level of "stickiness" that has allowed GitHub to quickly become an industry standard for software-development projects.

The environment is so efficient, it now encompasses not just code projects, but anything that involves working with files on a computer, from writing books to designing circuit board schematics.

The GitHub community is now self-sustaining, but is clearly tended by a corporate team that understands the dynamics of growth and does not allow its offerings to become stale or dated.

Upworthy

In June 2013, *Fast Company* called Upworthy, "The fastest growing media site of all time." Since Upworthy was only founded in March 2012, that is a powerful statement reflective of the rapid growth of the new media outlet that focuses solely on curating and sharing viral content.

In November 2013, Upworthy had 88 million unique hits in a single month, placing it just behind the older and better known Gawker Media Network. Explaining the growth strategies behind Upworthy's early success is no easy task since by its nature the site depends on the elusive quality of "going viral."

It is often said that growth hacking is much more an art than a science, which is quite clear in the Upworthy story. Early in its evolution, the site focused on election-year hype to gain traction, but was soon forced to pivot away from politics to sustain its momentum.

The problem was clear and inevitable. Once the election was over, so was the interest. Since no growth hack or traffic mechanism is ever permanent, this was an expected phenomenon. The election gained traffic for Upworthy, so the issue then became keeping and growing that base.

Now, the team of curators at Upworthy has a more set "formula" with which to work, even if that process is difficult to define outside of the team. They concentrate on visually driven material that is interesting, surprising, emotional, or compelling — or better yet, a combination of all of the above.

This is often a matter of "feel" rather than a metric-driven selection process. The Upworthy team knows that middle-aged woman are the group most likely to share content online, so they work in the principle that all content should NOT make your Mom shake her head.

Seven months after launch, Upworthy already had 9 million unique hits per month. Site designers concentrated on framing the content to make it more "clicky" for Facebook and other social media sharing, which is helpful, but the curators are perfectly frank when they admit that much of their success is based on luck.

Each piece of content chosen it evaluated for its ability to generate multiple levels of sharing. Facebook integration has been vital to Upworthy's reach, so much so that critics have suggested that if Facebook shuts Upworthy out in the future (after the fashion of Google's Panda and Penguin updates) the action could spell disaster for the viral service.

This is not to suggest, however, that Upworthy hasn't built in its own call to action elements. When visitors land on the site from whatever source, they are asked to become subscribers before they can view the content.

Mobile users also represent a critical channel of distribution. In July 2013, mobile traffic accounted for about 40% of Upworthy's unique visits. Four months later that level was up to 57%.

Continued refinement of the mobile reader will undoubtedly be central to Upworthy's growth strategy. Currently, about 63% of the traffic is U.S. based, and Upworthy is working on adapting their understanding of viral dynamics for other cultures and languages — no small proposition.

Whether Upworthy will prove to be a flash in the pan remains to be seen, but in the short term, they are a definite example of growth hacking as a unique mixture of market understanding and sheer luck.

Groupon

The deal-of-the-day website Groupon launched in November 2008 in Chicago. It now serves merchants in 500 markets spread over 48 countries. When the company filed for its IPO in 2010, it cited $713.4 million in revenue, up from $30.47 the previous year for a staggering growth rate of 2.241%.

How did they do it? By turning every user into a marketer. Sharing is so integral to the Groupon experience that it has been described as a strand of the site's "DNA," an element hardwired into the site's core concept.

Sharing on Groupon is largely motivated by self-interest. Consider this scenario. A user finds a great deal, but not enough people have signed up. Only half a dozen more and you can get that great price! What are you going to do? Tell your family and friends and followers and anyone else you can think of. You want the deal. Groupon wants the users. That's a huge win/win, a brilliant growth strategy for the site, and a point of leverage for businesses.

If a single purchase is a good offering, a package for multiple people is even better. The business attracts more interest and Groupon gets more potential users. As this ecosystem has evolved, it's an interesting mix of shared benefits with an element of chasing after bargains that deal hunters find irresistible.

Once a user has purchased a deal, Groupon sends them a daily email to keep them looking at offers without having to think about actually visiting the site. The ongoing contact is sufficiently low key as to not be perceived as inbox spam, which users hate. For emails to overcome the danger of being perceived as a nuisance, they must carry a real value proposition and be respectful. That's a difficult balance to strike, but Groupon does it right.

As if these strategies were not sufficient to turn every single Groupon user into growth promoters, there is also a referral system. For every referred user who actually buys a deal, the referrer earns $10.

Not surprisingly, since January 2010, the largest number of referrals to Groupon come from Facebook sharing activity. There is also the option to buy for a friend to give them a taste of the Groupon experience as a gift.

By optimizing opportunities for social sharing and offering high value deals, Groupon built a thriving user base that the company estimated at 42.6 million in June 2013. (That number reflects customers who purchased a deal in the previous 12 months.)

Facebook

As the largest and best recognized of all the social media networks, Facebook's rise to prominence has been nothing short of meteoric. The site was founded in 2004, reached 100 million users in 2008, and broke 1.11 billion members in March 2013.

It is generally accepted that Mark Zukerberg and his team were growth hacking before anyone was even using the phrase. Much of this was accomplished by a corporate culture unlike any other seen at the time.

Every employee at Facebook was involved in brainstorming the success of the endeavor. The constant drive was for easier, newer, better ways to enable participation via an intuitive interface that allowed for ease of sharing and a high viral reach.

This included making the social media platform available in as many different languages as possible. The funnel to draw in new users was incorporated at every level of the Facebook product.

Everyone at the company had to understand and use the product to sharpen their understanding of how the consumer would engage in the same activities.

No division within the Facebook internal structure was any more important than any other, and all were charged with the philosophy of KISS — keep it simple, stupid.

Although there have been notable departures along the way, with alterations to the look and feel of the interface that led to a user outcry, the Facebook team simply adjusts on the fly. They have no difficulty rolling out or rolling back changes.

There has consistently been a sharp focus on the design of the user experience, including an effort to remove distractions. One of the biggest innovations was replacing hyperlinked text with colored buttons when it was discovered that the buttons returned a higher rate of response.

Then, however, Facebook set about researching and testing how the buttons themselves worked, playing with image size, font choices, and colors. The quest became finding the most clickable button possible.

Calls to action on Facebook have built-in social pressure, which is why the "like" button was such a game changer. It is simple, low cost, and incredibly powerful.

As the user culture of Facebook developed, people began to feel compelled to "like" this or that item rather than appear disengaged in the lives of their friends. This subtle social pressure was highly instrumental in growing Facebook and remains so today.

Now, just as many people like and share the paid elements of the site and business content as they do the personal elements. Interestingly, there is also a growing demand for a "dislike" button.
Some users are particular about the curation of their newsfeed and others are not, but the point is that every 20 minutes on Facebook 1 million links are shared. In 2013, Facebook's revenue was $6,150,000,000.

The site is not just one of the great Internet success stories, but arguable *THE* great story. Although growth has slowed somewhat, there is no question but that Facebook is now self-sustaining, increasing its user base at a rate of about 22% per year.

Twitter

The micro-blogging site Twitter is a good example of perfect market fit, coming along at a time when society as a whole completely embraced rapid exchanges of bursts of information. This allowed Twitter to grow 1400% from February 2008 to February 2009.

The numbers of actual users acquired in this period are not precise, but in September 2009, Twitter was getting 58.4 million visitors both inside and outside the United States.

Almost all of the company's tactics were copied from the Facebook example, especially as they related to developing a simple interface that encouraged link sharing and social interaction.

Twitter, however, was specifically tailored for a mobile world where smartphones were rapidly gaining ascendancy. With a limit of just 140 characters, "tweets" inspired a new kind of expression that users found compelling.

It also gave celebrities a low-commitment venue to connect more personally with their fans. These famous adaptors were hugely instrumental in Twitter's growth. Millions of users followed Ashton Kutcher, Oprah Winfrey, and an up-and-coming U.S. senator named Barack Obama.

Other social media platforms and even television programs and news broadcasts began to incorporate tweets for the succinct pithiness of the individual updates.
In 2012, more than 1.1 million new accounts were being opened each day on Twitter and it remains one of the most growth-oriented of all the online member communities.

There are many things that drive the compelling nature of Twitter. It is a constant flow of updates. Users can dip it at any point and be entertained or engaged. There is no beginning or ending.

Mutuality is not required. One user can follow another independently with no reciprocal action needed. At sign-up, following suggested accounts is encouraged, and enhances new user engagement by giving them something to read immediately.

Even more importantly, the Twitter API was made easily available to developers so that there are more than 100,000 companion apps for the service from client readers to photo sharing services that enhance the user experience.

A tweet can be sent from a 20-year-old cell phone as a text message. There is no need to sit down at a computer. For this reason, Twitter seems to readily turn members into citizen journalists during news events and natural disasters.

This lends an unusual degree of social relevance to the community that has made it even more acceptable in the eyes of mainstream culture. For instance, much of the information that reached the west from the Arab Spring democracy movement (2010-2013) did so via Twitter.

Much of Twitter's success stems from the sweet spot of having found a perfect product idea for the time that paired exceptional built-in virality with high social relevance. Couple that with ease of use, and growth was all but guaranteed.

Instagram

The online photo and video-sharing social network Instagram launched in October 2010 and gained 100,000 users in one week. As of March 2014, there were 200 million active monthly users on the service, 70% of whom log in every day. On average, 60 million photos are posted each day.

Instagram entered the social media photo sphere with one unique proposition no other service was offering, and that was a stroke of genius. Users could apply filters to their photos to create unique images that made them look like better pictures than they actually were!

In short order, the "Instagrammed" photo took on the appeal of other, older "less is more" photographic styles like Lomography (analog photos created with a low-budged Russian made camera) and the old, ubiquitous Polaroids of the 1960s and 1970s.

This Instagram sub-culture was and is populated with tech-savvy users who are deeply into social media and who have phones with increasingly more sophisticated cameras. Consequently, as Instagram has grown, much of the content has become frankly artistic, which has served as a growth engine in and of itself.

Integration with Facebook, Twitter, and Flickr is built into the app in a cooperative rather than a competitive fashion so that sharing is simple and natural. Instagrams are now instantly recognized on the other platforms, which further encourages new member sign-ups. Social media users don't like to feel "left out."

On a technical level, the Instagram app is unusually fast, which in the beginning was a rare for a mobile app. This applies both to the processing and upload of photos, and to browsing the site itself. Designers made the decision to load content based on importance, not order, so users are constantly seeing the most engaging images in their feeds.

The app constantly notifies users of what it is doing, so there is no perception of anything being "stuck" or "hung up." Reassuring users has proven a small but critical improvement that makes them patient and relieves any friction.

Photo sharing applications always carry an inherent risk of creating a venue for pornographic or improper content. Instagram's designers opted to make all profiles public automatically and thus discouraging that kind of behavior.

They do not censor content overtly, but have quietly trained users to consciously separate or curate their content based on perceived public pressure, a strategy similar to that used by Facebook. In so doing, an overall confidence in the user assurance is bolstered for a higher level of comfort in the community.

There is, however, also a key element of luck in the Instagram instant success story. On the day the service launched, Twitter founder Jack Dorsey tweeted about it — to the more than one million people who follow him. In short order, Instagram was "app of the Day" on the iTunes store — and the rest is history.

In fact, the Instagram "look," which is tailored to a square photo format, has become so ubiquitous in the world of mobile photographer, the format has been emulated in a number of iPhone photo apps to increase the options for image sharing on Instagram itself. Most notable among these is the highly popular Hipstamatic.

Since Instagram users can choose existing photos from their photostream and upload them with no edits or filters, the door is wide open for the use of pictures taken or edited with other applications. In this case, imitation is not only the sincerest form of flattery, but an additional growth stream for Instagram via third party applications!

Eventbrite

The online ticketing service Eventbrite was founded in 2006 and has become the platform of choice for organizing small to medium events. It allows for promotion and registration, as well as ticket sales to track and monetize attendance. This all-in-one approach is both effective and well-designed, appealing to users on both ends of the process.

By 2009, the site was handling $100 million in gross ticket sales, but then it was used widely as a venue to book events held in conjunction with President Barack Obama's inauguration.

The exposure created by these events created an awareness of Eventbrite among an important population of event organizers. By 2010, the number of gross ticket sales processed through the service more than doubled, and in 2012 Eventbrite boasted 20 million users.

Event organizers have free access to the site, and send invitations to their guests, which inherently spreads more awareness of the service. Simple user familiarity then leads to additional bookings, meaning Eventbrite has a kind of inherent viral factor that is a particular sweet spot for growth.

Eventbrite also benefited enormously from spontaneous word of mouth on sites like Facebook, LinkedIn, and Twitter where people were simply telling colleagues and friends about scheduled events. In growth hacking circles, this is referred to as social commerce.

The principle is simple. People act in relation to what their friends are doing. Initially that kind of social sharing was a cut-and-paste proposition for organizers and attendees. As soon as Facebook became one of its top 10 traffic sources, however, Eventbrite integrated with Facebook Connect, and was, in fact, one of the first services to make the link.

Event sharing became a one-button process and Facebook shot up to become Eventbrite's number one traffic driver. This proves that tracking data and being responsive to customer behavior is an important aspect of growth hacking.

Eventbrite constantly collects, observes, experiments, and tests its user data to find trends like the Facebook sharing behavior. Once in possession of the data/insight, the proper response is to then use the material to further optimize the user experience.

In the best case scenario, however, optimization is never done at the expense of simplicity and functionality, however. Unlike previous online ticket systems, Eventbrite keeps everything simple and straightforward.

Publishing an event is intuitive and highly focused on the self-serve principle. The learning curve is very, very shallow. Additionally, organizers gain access to useful and fairly complex analytics.

Eventbrite allows organizers to see who is attending their event, which of their marketing channels are most effective, and which events are selling. For professional organizers, this is crucial data that can completely alter how they handle their next event.

The site makes money by charging 2.5% of the ticket price plus $0.99 per ticket, capping the fee at $9.95 per ticket. With more than 80% of its business centered in the United States, Eventbrite is now focused on growing its presence internationally

Tinder

Tinder, which describes itself as a "location-based social discovery app," is actually a dating service launched in September 2012. There is, however, a unique twist. Tinder's designers immediately grasped how scale relates to location and built an app that works on the principle of social proximity.

Scale is the driver behind this thought process. An app with 1,000 people using it over a widely dispersed geographic region for social engagement is nothing in the greater scheme of things. If, however, those users are all in the same spot and can actually walk across a room and meet one another, something huge happens on the local scale. That's the stuff of explosive word of mouth, which is exactly what happened with Tinder.

The service capitalized on what it knew would be a "wow" factor among early adopters by hosting frat parties at the University of Southern California. The "price" of admission was downloading the Tinder mobile app. In one night, they signed up hundreds of single people in a localized and geographically dense market – all of whom were talking about their Tinder experience the next morning.

The app itself keeps things as simple as possible. Users upload as many as five photos along with their first name, age, and an optional tagline. The app locates other users in the defined area and begins sending out "matches." To respond, recipients swipe right for "cute" and left if they're not interested.

The app was released in August 2012, made the iTunes Top 100 list in five months, and by summer 2014 had racked up 4.7 billion profile ratings and was the number one downloaded dating app in use.

Tinder's localized focus means that users are already part of groups or networks of people who have similar interests — like attending the same university. This creates a higher level of comfort about potential meetings and reaches out to social influencers with peer group status. Tinder gambled on organic word of mouth, but it was a calculated bet that paid off handsomely.

The app design also ensures that conversations only take place among interested parties, so the kind of spamming or trolling seen with other dating apps doesn't happen with Tinder. There is a built-in "walk away" element that women in particular find attractive. In this genre of software, a positive experience is a powerful growth driver, and in that regard, Tinder delivers.

The app is now available in 25 languages and has been offered free of charge for approximately 18 months. In April 2014, Barry Diller, the chairman of Tinder investors IAC/InterActiveCorp said in an interview with Bloomberg that future monetization options included subscriptions, advertising, and the freemium model, which would unlock premium futures to users for a fee.

The freemium model is the most likely fit for Tinder since the app itself has not seen any major changes during its short lifetime. One gamble designers always face is boredom. If an app is allowed to grow stale, users move on to something else.

Existing users who are already fans of any service rarely balk at paying a small fee for added features, however, and new users, excited about doing the "in" thing don't hesitate to buy either. They see the fee as the price of admission.

There's every indication that even with monetization, Tinder will continue to grow because it has captured the sweetest of all growth hacking prizes, virality.

Reddit

In 2005 Steve Huffman and Alexis Ohanian founded the social news site Reddit on an admittedly dishonest growth hacking strategy. They used hundreds of fake user accounts in those early days to populate their website.

The high-quality content contained in those first articles set an important tone for the site, however, and kept Reddit from appearing to be a virtual ghost town. It made no sense to launch an empty site based on reading and sharing content.

Self-population was both brilliant and very necessary. Early explorers saw what looked like a thriving amount of activity and were less intimidated about becoming involved themselves.

Reddit works around a community of registered users who can submit content in the form of direct links or text posts. Other registered users vote on the submissions, moving them up and down in rankings on the site. There is a strong emphasis on both quality and accuracy.

As of April 21, 2014, Reddit boasts 114.9 million unique visitors per month from 190 countries. They account for 5.38 billion monthly page views and were responsible for 56 billion page views in all of 2013.

The site has excellent "stickiness," with an average visit lasting more than 15 minutes. Maintaining and growing user engagement is fundamental to growth hacking, and

Reddit does an exceptionally good job in this area. People stay because they're interested, which further enhances the Reddit reputation and generates spontaneous word of mouth.

The news that users see when they go to Reddit is based on their personal preferences as generated through their history of voting stories up and down. The longer you use Reddit, the better the site understands what you want to read and gives you more tailored content as well as allowing you to see those stories best liked by the Reddit community as a whole.

In October 2006, Condé Nast purchased Reddit, which then passed to its parent company, Advanced Publications, in 2011. In 2008, "subreddits" were incorporated into the user experience, which are entries organized by interest.

They are very like threads in discussion boards and became an instant hit, drawing even more users to the site. One of the most popular of the subreddits is "Ask Me Anything" or "AMAs" for short.

Some of the past AMA participants include President Barack Obama, Madonna, Bill Gates, Stephen Colbert, Rachel Maddow, Larry King, Bill Nye, Al Gore, Roger Ebert, and Michael Bolton. President Obama's AMA brought so many visitors to Reddit in August 2012, many parts of the site crashed.

Built on a simple growth hack — make the site look active and popular — Reddit is now considered something of a growth hacker's paradise. Using subreddits to test product fit and to judge the size of a market has become a standard tactic among growth hackers trying out their strategies.

Once a "product market fit" has been discovered, Reddit can then be used for product promotion through an engine like an AMA. This is, however, a double-edged sword. The Reddit community, which began on a lie, now values absolute transparency. If a self-promoter of any kind starts an AMA and refuses to answer hard questions, they are likely to be savaged by the Reddit community.

AirBnB

The San Francisco company Airbnb was founded in August 2008. It currently has more than 500,000 listings for lodgings available for rent in 34,000 cities and 192 countries. A wide variety if spaces are included, from whole house to rooms and even some private islands!

The service's success was largely dependent on a brilliant albeit questionably ethical growth hacking strategy involving Craigslist. Before they were shut down, Airbnb had an option for users to cross post their available accommodation listings to Craigslist, which created inbound links both for the individual user, but also for the Airbnb platform.

This is one of the more infamous and technical of the "great" growth hacking stories, and worked brilliantly until AirBbB began to directly contact Craigslist users. Those people had no idea who or what AirBnB was and began to complain that the company was using a "black hat" hack.

The interactions AirBnB attempted to initiate were fairly aggressive, going out to Craigslist users who had specifically indicated they did not want to be contacted by commercial entities. While AirBnB was working outside of the Terms of Service for Craigslist, they characterized the relationship as "symbiotic."

This claim is highly semantic since Craigslist didn't offer a public API in 2009. The AirBnB hack was a reverse engineered stealth integration.

The engineers created a bot that automatically posted listings to Craigslist by logging in, acquiring a URL, filling in all the necessary information, and allowing the AirBnB user to hit the "post to CL" option.

The coding behind the hack was complex and capable of jumping through a number of hoops on the Craigslist end, including the default anonymous address provided to posters. Without a doubt, AirBnB knew that if they were caught, they'd be kicked off, which is exactly what happened.

They invested the time, money, and considerable programming resources to complete the hack anyway because they knew that by the time they were caught, they would already have captured their own user base and from that point could be self-sufficient.

It is not unusual for a start-up to leverage the power of an existing big platform. Just look at the success Zynga has had providing access to its games via Facebook. The difference is that AirBnB took a guerrilla approach to the "bootstrapping" and did so without the knowledge or consent of Craigslist.

Without question, the growth hack worked for AirBnB and it does illustrate the idea that all marketing techniques, including aggressive growth hacks, have a short lifespan. If, however, they can deliver big results before they "die," the strategy can still have merit so long as you don't completely compromise the reputation of your business in the process and lose user confidence.

This didn't happen in the case of AirBnB because the hack was so sophisticated, most users were unaware of it and didn't understand it if they became aware. In the tech community in 2009 this sort of maverick behavior was still reasonably common, so AirBnB had everything to gain and little to lose.

Dropbox

Dropbox is a cloud-based solution for file synchronization founded in 2007 and launched in 2008. The company's growth curve since 2011 has been steady and impressive:

- October 2011 - 50 million users
- November 2012 - 100 million users
- November 2013 - 200 million users

In the beginning, however, the standard "start-up" strategies didn't get Dropbox where it wanted to be. The company worked with a PR firm, bought ads on Google, and attempted to leverage social media — to the tune of almost $400 paid out for every new user acquired! Obviously with that kind of financial outlay, Dropbox was not going to be a success.

They went back to the drawing board and set out to figure out why the truly useful idea of cloud-based storage wasn't taking off. That's when the company realized that users didn't understand they actually did have the problem Dropbox was poised to solve.

Although brilliant in its design, the company had unwittingly put the cart before the horse. The average person didn't yet see the advantage of having access to their files from any connected device anywhere in the world.

The first task, therefore, in growing the Dropbox user base was educational. Their message, however, could not be directed solely at the tech savvy. The average person had to see and understand why they needed Dropbox and how they would use it to make their lives better. Simplicity was an absolute prerequisite for success.

First, designers completely overhauled the company's homepage so that the entire focus was on signing up. The implied message became, "This is so easy, so is using Dropbox." An embedded two-minute video explained how the service worked and prominently featured a bright blue download box.

Then, Dropbox made good on its promise. The sign up process is seamless and at the basic level, new users get 2 gb of free space, a pre-configured folder for their photos, and a text file on "getting started." The emphasis on photo storage is intentional and brilliant.

Every time a user installs the Dropbox app on a mobile device, automatic photo synchronization is offered as an option. Mobile users make heavy use of their built-in cameras.

The synchronization option cleverly capitalizes on the fear that photos might be lost along with the phone or tablet or that some images will have to be deleted to make room for others

The engineers at Dropbox understood that photographs carry a high level of emotional engagement. Users who might not see a need to synchronize documents will want to protect their images. Once they understand what

Dropbox can do for them, they see its value and want "in." These are also the kind of people who will willingly pay for additional storage space as their needs grow.

Dropbox has further plugged into that emotion by making it incredibly simple for users to share large photo files in shared folders by sending a simple link to family and friends.

Again, this is an instance of achieving market fit by understanding user needs. As the resolution of digital cameras has gone steadily up, users who have no file management or photo editing skills have experienced more and more difficulty sharing images.

Dropbox offers an easily understood solution that is also tied to new member sign-ups. If you want to see the pictures of your grandchildren, just sign up for this free account.

The company also uses a powerful referral system that increased signups by 60% when it was introduced. For each new user referred, the person offering the referral and the person referred each get an additional 500 mb of storage space. Friend referrals are always more powerful than advertisement because they carry the weight of a personal recommendation.

The offered incentives don't stop there. Just for linking a Facebook and Dropbox account users get 125 mb of space. The same holds true for Twitter linkage. Could something so simple work? Dropbox has 3.59 million followers on Twitter and more than a million likes on Facebook.

After a rocky start, Dropbox figured out what its potential users needed, identified the points of friction getting in the way, and adopted a philosophy of simplification and education. With that new focus, the year-over-year user numbers immediately began to double.

PayPal

PayPal is widely regarded as the most established of all the online payment solutions. Since its founding in 1998, the company has become an international e-commerce portal for payments and money transfers.

Early in its existence, however, PayPal literally paid for new customers, offering a $10 sign-up incentive as well as a $10 referral fee. Using this system, they achieved 7-10% daily growth, but was an expensive proposition and one that could not be sustained over the long term.

According to Eric M. Jackson in his 2012 book, *PayPal Wars*, the company, looking for a cheaper way to pull in new users, employed a hack not unlike the one AirBnB used to bootstrap Craigslist. The PayPal engineers wrote a bot that purchased good on eBay, but insisted that payment occur through PayPal.

This tactic allowed eBay sellers to become familiar with the PayPal service and drove them to sign up for accounts fearing they were missing out on something they perceived to be popular with their buyers.

Fortunately PayPal did work as advertised, which was a plus, but the strategy was still one of "fake it until you make it. Regardless, it worked – so well, in fact, that EBay purchased PayPal in 2002.

After the eBay acquisition, PayPal legitimately become the payment method of choice for auctions and sales. The symbiotic relationship was more than enough to sustain PayPal as a successful company. Although complacency is the bane of all growth hackers, PayPal more or less sat on its laurels.

The company did not experience another serious uptick in its user base until the second half of 2009 when site traffic tripled in six months.

Certainly a number of positive were in place for the company at the time, including user familiarity through eBay. Many people who had never used PayPal were still peripherally aware of its existence.

Additionally, the company was expanding its reach geographically and moving into the Asian sphere. It also released a multi-platform mobile payment app which became immediately popular with users. But the real growth mover was the release of a flexible API that gave developers access to the PayPal platform for incorporation into their own apps and websites.

Third-party developer support was the missing key in taking an already arguably successful company and moving it into its current prominence as the leading online payment system. The more places and context in which PayPal appears, the more its reach will grow.

Seen over the span of its 16 years in operation, making it a venerable senior citizen on the Internet, PayPal has used both "black hat" aggressive moves and shrewd market understanding to both achieve, sustain, and extend its growth.

All growth hackers counsel against any endeavor resting on its laurels, an anti-growth sin that PayPal has brilliantly avoided.

eBay

EBay was founded in 1995 to conduct the kind of business traditionally seen in venues like garage sales and flea markets but in an online environment accessible 24-hours a day. It was, in short, a dream for junk lovers the world over.

Now the site is a multi-billion dollar international business with a presence in 30 countries, but it began with the simple premise that one person's trash is another person's treasure. Case in point: the first item sold on eBay (when it was still known as AuctionWeb) was a broken laser pointer.

The arguably worthless item was posted as a test of the system, but received a winning bid of $14.83. When eBay founder Pierre Omidyar contacted the winner and asked if he knew the laser pointer didn't work, he received a succinct reply, "I'm a collector of broken laser pointers."

This rummage sale ethos alone was enough to make eBay profitable from year one. The site was quirky, and fun, and carried a high level of stickiness. Users loved to brose the auctions, a sales model that engaged their competitive juices and led them to bid on the listed items no matter how improbable they might be.

From the beginning, eBay achieved market fit in a well-defined niche and did quite well until a three-year period during the tenure of then CEO Meg Whitman. During that time the company's stock price dropped 50% and its market value declined by $30 billion.

Most critics agree that two actions in particular damaged the highly successful company during these years, the purchase of Internet telephone service Skype in September 2005 for $3.1 billion and a failed attempt to enter the China market.

Whitman retired from the company in 2008 and was succeeded by Jack Donahoe who was faced with re-growing an already successful, but then floundering company. One of the primary fundamentals of growth hacking is constant reassessment and redesign, which is exactly what Donahoe did.

He saw Skype as a distraction that brought no added value to the company, so he sold a 70% stake in the service to a private equity firm for $2.75 billion. This was the first step in re-honing eBay's commitment to the person-to-person sales that were its core vision in the beginning.

The effort began to pay off, as reflected in eBay's year-over-year growth figures:

- 2010 - 4.91%
- 2011 - 27.25%
- 2012 - 20.77%
- 2013 - 14.03%

The site has, however, continued to diverge from the original auction model since 2010 when fixed-price "Buy It Now" sales accounted for 59% of sales in the second quarter of the year. While this is a departure from the original eBay vision, the alteration reflects a major concern in the seller community that negatively affects their profit potential.

An auction can either yield high returns or allow a valuable item to disappointingly sell for very little money. If free-shipping is also offered on the item, the seller is then in a position to lose money and operate in the red.

Although a "Buy It Now" sale takes longer, there's a higher chance of making a good sale, which encourages more listings – the lifeblood of the eBay concept.

Mobile retailing is also a powerful driver for sales. There have been more than 90 million downloads of the eBay mobile app, which, in tandem with payment via PayPal, has revolutionized how people shop. This is a natural outgrowth of the widespread adoption of smartphones, a trend further buoyed by the tablet computer phenomenon.

PayPal is an example of one of many strategic acquisitions eBay has made over the years that has buoyed the site's core functionality while helping to shut out competitors.

EBay bought PayPal in 2002 for what then seemed like an outrageous $1.5 billion, but now looks like a bargain with the new emphasis on mobile commerce. Shoppers can browse for items and pay for them on their phones or tablets with just a few clicks, desktop no computer or laptop required.

Along these same lines, eBay bought the mobile payment company Braintree in September 2013 for $800 million. The company's Venmo app enables instant money wires to friend's bank accounts from smartphones. EBay plans to merge that technology with PayPal to create even more seamless mobile payments.

These targeted acquisitions that edge eBay closer and closer to real market fit are a much better use of corporate resources and have successfully pulled eBay back from decline to its current position as the Internet's premier selling site.

Warby Parker

Warby Parker is primarily an online seller of prescription eyewear, although it has a few bricks-and-mortar locations. Frames are designed in-house, with most selling for $95.

Since its founding in 2010, the brand has distinguished itself for its often quirky but thoroughly engaging approach to customer satisfaction. For instance, the Home-Try-On program allows customers to receive five frames to try at home for five days at no cost.

Warby Parker also exhibits an appealing a social conscience. For each pair of glasses they sell, they pay for the production of a second pair to be given to an individual in need through the non-profit VisionSpring.

Warby Parker has been responsible for the distribution of almost half a million pairs of glasses through this relationship. Beyond being a genuinely charitable endeavor, the strategy is a subtle reinforcement of the company's "vision" both as product and corporate culture.

But the real growth engines at Warby Parker are social engagement and virality. More than 50% of the company's sales are achieved via word of mouth generated through diversified use of social media and email.

The company utilizes Tumblr and Pinterest primarily for brand awareness while it interacts with consumers in real time on Twitter and Facebook. The content on these feeds is quirky and has extreme viral appeal.

For instance, Warby Parker maintained a Pinterest board that was originally called "Bespectacled Bloggers," but is now "Our Friends in Our Frames." It contains 218 pins and has 13,217 followers.

The company sees email as a tool for personal engagement. Responses to customers include links to silly videos, funny comments, and options for social sharing.

On average, an email from Warby Parker is shared up to 80 times! The company knows that mobile device users are increasingly watching video content wherever they may be, so all content is optimized for mobile sharing.

Warby Parker has managed to create a corporate culture that makes it stand out from the crowd and attract a loyal following. While this approach won't necessarily work for every product or every company, it is an excellent example branding to achieve growth.

YouTube

YouTube, the now ubiquitous video-sharing site, was founded in 2005 and acquired by Google in 2006 for $1.65 billion. The site immediately became one of the fastest growing destinations online. By July 2006, there were 65,000 videos uploaded per day that generated 100 million views.

By 2014, some 1 billion YouTube users post 100 hours of video content per minute. The average user spends almost eight hours a month on the site, which reaches more adults age 18-34 in the United States than any cable network.

YouTube's success can be traced to its multi-level appeal. It is a social network like Facebook in that users can follow one another, comment on video content, create playlists, and publish their own channels. At the same time, channels can be used as an advertising platform or for the pure delivery of content.

A YouTube channel is an "everyman's" venue to publishing video content that, if it goes viral, can be a ticket to a music career, acting roles, or television or movie contracts. For some, YouTube has literally been a place where dreams come true.

It began, however, in a garage in Menlo Park, California. Three former PayPal employees wanted to share some video of a party the night before. They weren't sure how to do it, so they started brainstorming, bought a domain name, spent some months developing the site, and released a public beta in May 2005 populated with videos of PJ, a cat that belonged to one of the founders.

Initially they tried to create buzz by giving away an iPod Nano to a random user every day for two months, but in the end, their connections may have been their greatest asset.

The former CFO of PayPal, Roelof Botha ran into YouTube founder Steve Chen at a party. They talked about the new site, and Botha posted clips of his Italian honeymoon. Word of mouth in the tech community picked up, and Botha started to look at YouTube as a potential investment.

The YouTube story is a curious mixture of a solution that solved a specific problem (efficiently sharing video content in an accessible way), luck (knowing the right people), and virality.

The proliferation of camera phones drove the success of photo posting sites like Instagram and social sharing on Facebook and Twitter, but users were at something of a loss about what to do with their phone's video capability.

Emailing large files multiple times was too bulky, there were always issues with compatibility, and far too much overall friction for the experience to be enjoyable.

YouTube solved all those problems, and instantly began to capitalize on other social media sites by making sharing to Facebook, Twitter, and a host of other sites a one click proposition.

Now, YouTube content is so enmeshed in the social commerce inherent in those sites, that it is, itself, a growth hacking engine for emerging sites seeking a channel to create viral videos.

Mint

Mint is a free web-based service for financial management available to users in the United States and Canada. It was created in 2006 by Aaron Patzer and is now a subsidiary of Intuit, the makers of Quicken and TurboTax.

Mint allows users to connect with more than 16,000 financial institutions and supports more than 17 million individual financial accounts. In 2013, the service claimed more than 10 million users.

The greatest challenge to growth faced by Mint was in creating sufficient confidence in the site's security that its users would enter sensitive financial details into the interface with confidence. Much of Mint's growth hacking focus was geared toward addressing this primary concern.

First, the Mint staff became experts in online finance, researching not only the competition, but also the behavior of their potential users in regard to money. They discovered that most people do not track their income or their spending, preferring instead to simply keep an eye on their balances.

While most people understand the concept of budgeting, few implement it, or even know how to begin to do so, even though they might believe that there are real benefits to be derived from doing so.

This understanding allowed the Mint growth hackers to opt to focus on people who did not yet see the necessity of organizing their financial lives. This meant grabbing the attention of users who were just signing up to "kick the tires."

The site's programmers engineered the interface so that within 5 minutes of a new user signing on, they were looking at a full graphical picture of the current state of their finances, with advice on how to build their money — all for free.

The site was, and is, clean and simple with an easy, short domain name. The early marketing emphasis was on winning the approval of tech savvy reviewers from Tech Crunch and Hacker News who would tout the site's security and utility, which helped Mint to "go viral."

In conjunction with the main site, Mint dispenses valuable information on personal finance through a companion blog. Instead of dry, boring text, the data is presented in eye-catching and easily understood info graphics that are actually instructional and helped, in the beginning, to spread the word about Mint as both a product and a learning tool.

The primary growth hacking strategies Mint employed worked with a brilliant combination of content marketing, product development, and behavioral engineering.

They found out who needed the product, how to gain the attention of early adopters, and how to give these people tools to reach a desirable goal — greater financial security and wealth accumulation.

These strategies allowed Mint to become the personal financial tool of choice for millions of users, even outpacing the tried and true Excel spreadsheet. Excel simply tracks financial data, Mint tracks data and educates its users in the process - a powerful and useful combination.

Udemy

Udemy, a web-based platform for online learning, was founded in 2010 and currently offers more than 16,000 courses. The bulk of the classes are not certified, but are offered for self-improvement only. Some coursework can be applied for technical certification, but no courses are currently eligible to convert to college credits.

With the provided tools, any user can design and create a course, promote it for student registration, and earn money from the collection "tuition." As of May 2014, Udemy experienced a 300% rate of growth over 12 months and successfully raised $48 million in financing for future expansion.

In the beginning, lack of content presented the greatest challenge to Udemy's growth. Like the Reddit team, Udemy's growth hackers had no choice but to seed the site themselves with courses from the OpenCourseWare movement that carried a creative common license. (OpenCourseWare content is course materials created at major universities and published for free use online.)

Thus, Udemy could legitimately say that its first 100 courses originated from prestigious universities like Stanford, MIT, and Yale. When the site launched with coverage on influential sites like TechCrunch and Mashable, they gained approximately 10,000 users.

Although this success was not sufficient to achieve the desired levels of growth, it did prove the concept and created an initial pool of users. This was enough to raise $1 million in seed money and allowed the finders to keep the ship afloat as they worked on recruiting experts, experienced academics, and authors to become instructors.

This involved hours of one-on-one meetings via Skype, but no real exciting content was forthcoming until the Udemy founders hit on the idea of filming a series of meetings with their own investors.

The "Raising Capital for Startups" course took off and led to the creation of two more offerings in the same format. Each one earned $30,000 to $50,000 and gave Udemy real traction with potential instructors.

From there, Udemy's engineers became tightly focused on offering the best tools and technology possible to facilitate online instruction. The value of teaching a course online had been proven, with optimization of the process being the next logical, and necessary step.

Teachers of all kinds are accustomed to making low wages, so the site had to offer high value to the very people it needed to grow. In May 2013, Udemy was able to report that its top 10 instructors generated more than $1.6 million in course sales.

Although wildly successful now, Udemy was faced with the task of gaining early adopters and creating initial success stories to drive subsequent waves of development.

At each phase, the team reevaluated what was necessary for the next level of growth to be obtained until the site reached a self-sustaining level of customer satisfaction, high quality content, word of mouth, and demonstrable earnings.

TripAdvisor

TripAdvisor was founded in 2000 to provide users with a directory of travel related information as well as mechanisms for hotel and flight booking, vacation rentals, and travel guide materials along with user-generated reviews.

In March 2013, *Forbes* reported more than 75 million user reviews were housed on the TripAdvisor site, which was garnering 62 million unique visits per month. Of those, 45 million were generated from mobile devices.

Those figures are an impressive upsurge from the 32 million unique monthlies tallied in 2008, but like many start-ups, TripAdvisor had virtually no traffic in the beginning, especially after 9/11 decimated the travel industry.

Then, the site changed its model to cost per click or CPC. When a consumer clicked on a hotel and booked a room, TripAdvisor charged the hotel. No clicks, no charges. In three months, the company that had been earning nothing was pulling in $70,000 per month.

By making this subtle change, TripAdvisor grew their own user base while also catering to the needs of the struggling travel industry. They made advertising through membership more affordable, so both sides benefited.

All TripAdvisor site development then became focused on customer engagement to increase the number of profitable clicks. Editors were hired to bring in travel articles, and users were allowed and encouraged to post reviews of their personal travel experiences.

When the reviews themselves begin to draw in the most site traffic, TripAdvisor shifted gears again to focus on review generation. This ensured a steady supply of fresh and honest content. The more trusted the perception of the TripAdvisor reviews, the more users posted.

In 2004, the company was bought by Expedia/IAC for $210 million in cash, an amazing accomplishment since they had raised only $4 million in venture capital. TripAdvisor continued to grow under the Expedia umbrella, and was spun back out as an independent company in 2011.

The heart of the success enjoyed by TripAdvisor lies in the belief that free content generated voluntarily by users carries the highest level of credibility and will generate the most profitable site activity.

This is a model not unlike that used by Hubspot to achieve growth. It represents good use of market fit since travel always carries the potential risk of a bad experience in multiple venues. Who hasn't been afraid of staying in a flea bag hotel or paying through the nose for an awful meal at a restaurant?

As the repository of reviews at TripAdvisor has grown both in numbers and in depth, the "stickiness" of the site has increased. Users don't just go to TripAdvisor to book, but also to plan. They research venues, often returning multiple times as they refine their vacation and travel plans. The longer a user stays on the site, the greater the chance they will click and make a reservation.

This is a very network-driven approach to growth, but one that proved highly successful for all parties concerned: the consumer, the advertised venues, and the hosting platform.

Goodreads

Software engineer and voracious reader Otis Chandler launched Goodreads in 2006. The site is now the leading online community for readers, but even in the first year it attracted 100,000 members for the simple reason that people who read books love to talk about books.

While that is market fit at its most simplistic, many bookcentric websites have failed. Goodreads did not thanks to Chandler's acumen both as a bibliophile and a technocrat.

Goodread's initial growth strategies included the development of a Facebook app, widgets for placements on blogs and websites, and integration with Twitter. Word of mouth, however, was key to the site's long term success.

As Chandler himself said, "Reading may be a solitary activity, but what you're reading and what you think of what you're reading are ideas. And ideas are much better if they're shared."

That simple idea, that is the meeting place between reading and social networks was the magic ingredient, sharing -- more specifically, creating the desire to share and providing the tools to do so effortlessly.

The site also immediately offered and gained targeted advertising from authors and publishers through a clever means of quantification. Users "shelved" books they had read and placed the ones they planned to get to on their "to read" lists. That activity was close enough to actual "intent to buy" to attract advertising revenue.

Simply plugging into the word of mouth that is an inherent part of any community of readers allowed Goodreads to expand to 16 million members by the time it was purchased by Amazon in March 2013.

By then, the site included reviews, book clubs, thriving discussion groups and threads, and even trivia games. Eleven months after the Amazon purchase, Goodreads had packed on another 4 million users thanks in large part to explosive mobile growth.

That's not surprising since Amazon merged Goodreads participation into the interface of its popular Kindle line of readers. Within the text of a Kindle book, if a reader highlights a passage, they are prompted to share their "thought" on Goodreads, with options to also post to Twitter and Facebook.

At the end of the book, the reader is immediately prompted to rate the title on Goodreads and to post a review if they so desire. This integration eliminates the thought process, "I should go to Goodreads and post this," which involves conscience effort. If the option is right there on the screen the chances for spontaneous activity on Goodreads is much higher – and it works.

Goodreads now has a repository of more than 25 million book reviews, which will no doubt expand rapidly thanks to the Kindle integration. With so much information in one place and ease of mobile access, members can seek out opinions and recommendations about books they're interested in purchasing while they're standing in a bookstore.

This is an even more powerful driver for publishers and authors to buy advertising space on the site. Not surprisingly, Goodreads is considered one of the "go to" self-promotion venues for the rising class of self-published authors that are rapidly turning the book world on it sear.

As a voracious reader himself, Otis Chandler came into the development of Goodreads with an intuitive understanding of market fit bolstered by his tech acumen as a software engineer. The combination proved highly effective and made Goodreads a prime prospective partner for Amazon's continuously evolving book/reader ecosystem.

Waze

The free turn-by-turn navigation app Waze debuted in Israel in 2008 and in six years became a worldwide phenomenon that has redefined how people cope with one of the greatest headaches of the modern world — traffic.

The app provides layers of information on top of digital maps that help drivers avoid traffic snarls. These include the location of road work, car accidents, and law enforcement speed traps as well as extras like the location of the cheapest gas available on a driver's given route.

The company's stated goal is to shave at least 5 minutes off every user's daily travel time with community-edited maps that are constantly being updated and improved. In today's modern world, that's a value proposition that requires no further explanation.

The app is both useful and fun, taking many cues from the world of gaming, which has help to speed adoption. Users who report any kind of traffic or map data get points that are currently used to define status and rank within the Waze system. Values vary.

Some examples include road reporting, which garners 6 points per report, while a gas price report is worth eight. Adding house numbers is only a 1 point action, but new road recording is worth 64. Drivers who clock off 500 miles in a week get 1000 points.

(New roads can be added through a manual interface from the Waze website for the cartographically obsessed, or users can simply turn on the "pave road" function in the app and drive. No roads are officially added to the service, however, until a map editor has confirmed their accuracy.)

Even though there is no monetary benefit (beyond cheap gas) associated with point generation, running up the totals appeals to naturally competitive users who want to go from being a "Waze Baby" to "Waze Royalty."

In fact, all the functionality within Waze is designed to elicit a feeling of community and a sense of camaraderie in building maps and defeating the modern scourge of the traffic jam.

Arguably, the design of the app itself is the greatest growth hack of all. Waze is, in essence, a real-time game that generates an incredibly useful product — constantly updated maps that reflect real world travel conditions.

In July 2012, Waze announced it had built a user base of 20 million drivers — 10 million of those added in the prior 6 months. At that time, drivers using the app had travelled more than 3.2 billion miles.

In June 2013, Google purchased Waze for a reported $1.3 billion amid rumors that automakers were considering incorporating the mapping app into their GPS systems.

GrubHub

GrubHub, an online food ordering company founded in 2004, is an excellent example of success built on continuous innovation in response to customer's needs.

In the beginning, the site did nothing but list restaurants in the user's area that would deliver. The service ran on a freemium model. All restaurants in the area were listed, but those that subscribed were given premium placement.

As more restaurants began to sign up, many wanted to know if GrubHub planned to add online ordering functionality. The company began to use each new subscription sale as a way to refine their product, even going to far as to offer discounts to restaurants in exchange for feedback.

The preference of the customer dictated the evolution of the product, leading to a major strategy change away from subscriptions in 2006. Restaurant owners preferred a commission based approach, paying only when they actually made money through their listing via orders.

All restaurants were still listed, with preferential placement going to those that agreed to online ordering.

As GrubHub continued to evolve and learn from its customers, new options were added like a mobile app, coupon offerings, filters to highlight specific cuisines, and other sorting features.

In its 2014 filing for an IPO, GrubHub touted at 67% growth rate, which some critics have labeled misleading. Regardless, the service has menus for more than 250,000 restaurants, with ordering options for approximately 20,000 in more than 500 cities.

The company continues to innovate, and recently released a dedicated tablet-based service called OrderHub to allow restaurant owners real-time management capability for their digital pickup and delivery orders.

Quora

The question and answer site Quora was founded in 2009 and went public in 2010. It was created by two Facebook alums, Adam D'Angelo and Charlie Cheever, who were in a unique position to bring growth insight to the endeavor.

After coverage from *TechCrunch* on January 5, 2011, Quora enjoyed a social media surge, going from 3,000 Twitter mentions to more than 10,000 in a day. Seizing the moment, Quora deployed a growth team to keep the sudden influx of new users and to grow their base.

None of the growth hacking techniques the company applied are in any way revolutionary, but all were perfectly executed examples of taking and applying the fundamentals repeatedly to maximize success.

This "wash, rinse, repeat" model is key to growth applications since it tends to return compounding results, much like interest earned on a savings account or certificate of deposit.

Quora's engagement with users is razor sharp and aimed at "stickiness" to lengthen the period of time a person spends on the site. The goal is to get people hooked on relevant information.

To achieve this, Quora has crafted an excellent algorithm to suggest new and related questions to readers as well as those that are interesting and relevant based on the individual's browsing history.

The site does not rely on its users to actual read the content however, understanding that in spite of the text intensive nature of the web, many people prefer to watch video. Many Quora answers are also accompanied by short instructional videos of exceptionally high quality.

Having been created by two former Facebook employees, Quora has benefited from tightly integrated social media integration from its inception. When answering questions, members have the option to share the content on various platforms or through email, and they can share questions they've read as well.

Finding your friends on Quora is functional and easy, which enhances the social reach of the site and creates a greater sense of community. Inherent in any site that depends on a social component is the phenomenon of perceived status within the group, an especially strong driver on a question and answer site.

Relevancy is central to the Quora experience. Users can follow question threads and are updated in email when a new answer is added. (There is an option for a daily digest to avoid cluttering up the user's email inbox.)

On their custom home page, members can see the activity on threads they have followed, as well as new answer written by specific people they follow or content they have "up voted," which is the site's social bookmarking feature.

In January 2011, before the boost in traffic generated by the TechCrunch coverage, Quora had approximately 500,000 users. In July 2012, the site was averaging 1.5 million unique visits.

Given the presence of many luminaries and celebrities in a range of fields on the site, there is every indication the Quora ecosystem will continue to thrive and grow. It has, however, reached a self-sustaining mass and is unlikely to see another growth surge like the one in 2011.

Mixpanel

The analytics company Mixpanel, founded in 2009, has its rightful place in a book about growth hacking not only because it is itself a success story, but because it has become an essential growth hacking tool.

As the founder and CEO Suhail Doshi told Liz Gannes of *All Things D* in May 2012, "Analytics won't tell you what product to build. It will give you hypotheses, but you still have to have ideas."

Ryan Lawler, in a July 29, 2013 post for *TechCrunch*, "Now Analyzing More Than 15 Billion Actions a Month, Mixpanel

Launches a Big Marketing Campaign and a Conference About Analystics," described the company's usefulness this way:

"If you haven't been paying much attention to Mixpanel, that's probably because analytics are pretty boring . . . But if you are in the guru/ninja/growth-hacking business, you probably have at least one of your four displays tuned to Mixpanel all day long while you sip $5 locally roasted fair trade coffee and rub your beard and say to yourself, 'Hrm, interesting.'"

As of Lawler's writing, 1,300 mobile apps and websites were paying to use the Mixpanel platform to analyze more than 15 billion actions each month — and adding an additional billion month over month!

Mixpanel's growth is attributable to its unique approach to analytics. The data it tracks is unusually queriable due to the manner in which it's stored. There's a direct emphasis on funnel analysis to explain just where users are originating, and then on cohort analysis and retention. What happens with users after they reach a site?

With its highly customizable data reporting and sharply targeted usefulness to growth hackers themselves, Mixpanel is a pretty clear cut case of perfect market fit.

From its initial $500,000 seed money financing to successive rounds of funding well into the millions, Mixpanel has not gone begging.

In the wake of a $10 million funding deal in May 2012 Doshi told VentureBeat, "Mixpanel has been cashflow positive for a while, so we weren't in a hurry to raise funding."

TaskRabbit

The online and mobile marketplace TaskRabbit was launched in 2008 in Boston as "RunMyErrand." It became TaskRabbit in 2010 to avoid perceived limitations in the word "errand" and to go with a name that was more memorable and fun. At the same time, the base of operations was changed to San Francisco.

TaskRabbit is a venue for outsourcing small neighborhood jobs to pre-approved "TaskRabbits" who compete for job listings that describe the required task and give an offered price or ask for bids. Dropping the word "errand" from the service's name helped branding.

While users might hire someone to run to the grocery store for them, the job might also be assembling a shelving unit or organizing a closet. The more all-encompassing word "task" was chosen to open up user's imagination about why and how they might utilize the service.

In May 2011, TaskRabbit secured $5 million in financing with 2,000 TaskRabbits proving the concept was workable. Over the course of a year, the service expanded into four more markets: New York City, Chicago, Los Angeles, and Orange County and also launched a mobile app.

A second round of funding to the tune of $17.8 million in December 2011 allowed the company to focus on their product development, including incorporating a gamified approach. Top workers are ranked on a leader board that also displays their average customer reviews.

This kind of peer-to-peer sharing involves crafting a perception of trust so users are willing to do business with strangers. Each potential TaskRabbit is given a criminal background check and interviewed via video before they are approved.

The site design emphasizes this guarantee, "Find safe, reliable help in your neighborhood" from "20,000+ Background Checked TaskRabbits." Sign-up is free and requires only an email address and a zip code, a dead simple method taken from the playbook of highly successful buy low-key sites like DropBox.

TaskRabbit founder Leah Busque advocates staying in constant update mode to make sure that users are always having the best possible experience with the product. Every two weeks the company tests its site design, user experience, and other features with A/B testing through Kissmetrics.

For instance, the company studies the effectiveness of photos versus illustrations on the front page and determined that photos result in twice as many sign-up.

There is a strong emphasis on the company's culture to ensure that everyone hired reflects the quality of the brand. TaskRabbit values openness with a helpful, collaborative, and friendly approach.

This is even bolstered by a selection of offices with open floor plans and the inclusion of a recreation room to inject some fun in the work place.

The reasoning is that the idea of TaskRabbit, though useful, is also quirkily and fun. Staying focused on the brand and offering the highest level of user experience possible has allowed this startup to thrive even in the face of competition.

Amazon

Amazon.com, founded in 1994, is the largest online retailer in the world. Originally, the site sold only books, but as its offerings have diversified, virtually anything can now be purchased through its online stores.

Additionally, the company produces a popular line of Kindle ebook readers that is largely credited with helping the digital book format to explode in popularity in recent years.

Before the site was ever launched, Amazon founder Jeff Bezos, attracted by the then projected web commerce growth of 2300%, analyzed the potential for various items to be sold online. He settled on books due to historic demand, low inventory price points, and the large number of titles in print.

Within two months, Amazon's sales reached $20,000 a week, a degree of success no doubt aided by Bezos' friendship with John Ingram of the Ingram Content Group, the largest distributor of books in the world.

In the first six months of operation, Amazon sold $500,000 worth of books. Five years later revenue hit $1.6 billion, and in 2013 the number skyrocketed to $17.09 billion.

There is no question that the site is popular and successful. In fact, the name Amazon is now synonymous with buying online, but the one thing that has consistently eluded the company is profit.

Bezos was clearly correct in his initial assessment of market fit, and the company has gone on to include the products he initially rejected as the basis for his business: CD/DVDs, computer hardware/software, and videos, plus much, much more.

In fact, Amazon has consistently worked to expand its market fit and reach. The company's closely integrated business model attempts to remove friction from the online buying process while offering exceptional value in pricing and item choice.

There is an optional "one-click" shopping button linked to a credit card associated with a user's profile. Orders of more than $25 ship free. If the user is a member of the Amazon

Prime program, all qualifying products receive free two-day shipping. Amazon clearly proves the assertion that the easier the shopping experience, the more the individual user will purchase.

Prime membership also gives users access to thousands of hours of free streaming video. Both movies and television programs are available for purchase and are stored in the user's online video library, as is purchased music. As more and more mobile users are becoming accustomed to streaming content from their devices, this is an excellent value-added proposition for the Prime subscription.

Side-by-side with its offering of new books, Amazon allows sellers to market used books and small businesses can apply to sell their items on the site as well.

While not as robust or active a small business climate as eBay or Etsy, the potential to earn money with sales on Amazon does still exist and given the size of the marketplace is attractive to individual entrepreneurs.

The Amazon API has long been available to outside sources so products listed on the company site can be sold elsewhere on the web, with the poster earning small commissions on each sale.

Through the company's companion Createspace and KDP sites, authors can self-publish their works in both paper and electronic formats. For ebooks published for the Kindle priced from $2.99-$9.99, authors earn 70% royalties.

Is the lack of profitability in the face of such variety evidence that Amazon is trying to do too much? That it cannot be all things to all people? Or is it simply an obstacle to be overcome on the way to building what has now become in Jeff Bezos' mind an online content ecosphere?

Critics are sharply divided in their answers, but one thing is clear. If you do your market research as Bezos did, and if you offer a quality users experience with a high value proposition and low friction, you can grow your site. In the days leading up to Christmas 2013, Amazon sold 426 items per second!

The Amazon Prime program has a membership of approximately 20 million and the site attracts more than 65 million customers in the United States alone each month. Amazon maintains stores that service Asia, Europe, North and South America, and Australia.

And, without question, Amazon does continue to innovate in proper growth hacker fashion. The company is experimenting with drone delivery and beginning to roll out one-day shipping in select markets. In the first quarter of 2014, Amazon's revenue grew 23%, edging the company every closer to its long-sought-after profitability.

RelayRides

RelayRides launched as a peer-to-peer service for car sharing in Boston during the summer of 2010. Originally it allowed participating car owners to offer their vehicles as rentals by the hour, day, or week. Late in 2010 the service expanded into the San Francisco area and then went nationwide in March 2012.

Early on the company benefited from $19 million in seed money from venture capitalists like General Motors and Google. Those funds were used to create brand awareness and acquisition of both car owners and renters. Much of this early activity was fairly standard TV and digital video ads paired with a search-based ad presence.

The idea was sufficiently attractive that during the summer of 2012 RelayRides expanded its total fleet by a factor of 40 with reservation volume expanding seven times. This allowed the company to have a presence in 49 states.

Based on market testing, they launched an experimental variant of the service at San Francisco International Airport. At the time, the goal was to stand out from the competition, but what happened so polished the value proposition of their market fit that RelayRides completely changed their focus to achieve maximum growth.

In looking at what users wanted, the RelayRides team zeroed in on the problem of transportation to and from airports. Traditionally, travelers could have the maximum degree of control over their own departures and arrivals by leaving their own cars at the airport, but rising parking expenses over the past few years have increasingly made that an exorbitant option.

RelayRides users drop their cars off at a parking lot and are taken to their terminal in a shuttle. Arriving members rent the cars for use, returning them to the lot when they leave. All vehicles receive complimentary car washes in between trips. This model sent membership soaring and the service spread to 229 airports.

In September 2013, the company announced that it would focus exclusively on long-duration car rentals since 95% of their revenues were being generated by that source. Customers on both ends of the equation love the option.

Renters pay 40% less for a RelayRides vehicle over a traditional rent car and the average vehicle owner makes $250 a month in profit. Some owners are so attracted to the concept, they put from 2-4 cars into service.

In studying the transportation/ride share market as part of the new economy of sharing, RelayRides hit on the untapped resource of underutilized vehicles that spend most of their time in the garage or parking lot.

As a facilitator of the owner/rental connection, the company takes 25% and in exchange provides $1 million of insurance on the vehicle during the rental period.

To assuage safety concerns, background checks are performed on participating owners and vehicle registration is verified. It also looks at the driving and safety records of prospective renters.

Again, this is an excellent example of impressive growth based on intuitive and extensive market research with ongoing testing in place to keep the company poised for a course direction to meet user needs. RelayRides has used basic but powerful growth hacking strategies and is reaping the rewards.

LivingSocial

LivingSocial launched in 2007 at roughly the same time Facebook got started. Founders Tim O'Shaughnessy, Aaron Batalion, Eddie Frederick, and Val Aleksenko saw the advent of the social network as an opportunity to acquire users quickly and inexpensively.

They tested this theory by creating a book-sharing application on Facebook called Virtual Bookshelf, which in its heyday had more book reviews than Amazon. Their next effort was LivingSocial, which in its first iteration simply asked users what they liked to do in real life and matched them with events in their area.

By going to a Facebook where they knew they could mine users, the LivingSocial founders were able to think out and refine their concept through testing. There really was no set plan for the direction of the business, which allowed them to tinker with their products, assemble a team, and follow what revenue was coming in.

They focused on brand awareness, user acquisition, and expansion. As they began to really develop a more coherent model, they poured all their resources into driving and refining it. What evolved out of those experiments was LivingSocial as it is known today, a local marketplace offering event tickets, vouchers, and gift certificates in the United States and 16 other countries.

The site has an estimated 70 million users and is, at its heart, a marketing platform to connect consumers and merchants through promotional offers. In any given area, about 55% to 65% of LivingSocial's business will be with local businesses.

Through mining user data, Living Social is very good at targeting which consumers that merchants are most likely to reach. If a business needs to bring in 500 customers in one week, a featured email is likely the best option, but if the goal is five customers a week for 30 weeks, the quota can be reached within the marketplace. Measurable results for merchants are one of the best ways to keep existing business and enhance word of mouth referrals.

LivingSocial is also one of the largest online resources for consumers to purchase tickets to live events. Through relationships with exhibitors, the company maintains an inventory of tickets and is often the exclusive seller for an events pre-sale campaigns.

In 2013, the company brought in almost $400 million in revenue on $1 billion in sales in spite of events that caused a crisis of confidence among its users. In April, some 50 million user records were hacked exposing encrypted passwords and email addresses, but not credit card information. Still, users were forced to reset their passwords.

In multiple interviews, CEO Tim O'Shaughnessy expressed optimism going into 2014, however, and continued to talk like a growth hacker. LivingSocial plans to become more of a destination via mobile apps and cultivate a searchable database of long-term deals that will appeal to users.

A platform re-design allows business owners to now manage multiple discount campaigns from one account, which should help strengthen LivingSocial's client relationships. Also, deal pages on the site are undergoing optimization to rank higher in searchers.

It is to LivingSocial's benefit that the company has had a strong growth culture from day one and is prepared to test and redesign key elements of its infrastructure to enhance both the user and customer experience. Although facing stiff competition from Groupon, LivingSocial is still very much in the game and well positioned for even greater growth.

Sidecar

Defining the prevailing zeitgeist at any moment in time can be a powerful but difficult growth hack, but San Francisco-based Sidecar, a major competitor with Uber in the sector of peer-to-peer ride sharing seems to be a good market fit for the rapidly emerging Sharing Economy.

In the months following its January 2012 launch in San Francisco, the company experienced 60% month-over-month growth and secured impressive funding starting with $20 million in seed money.

Like Uber, SideCar opted for a "proof is in the pudding" approach to demonstrating its value at the influential SXSW tech conference in Austin, Texas from March 8-17, 2013. All rides during the conference were free, and drivers were paid as brand ambassadors.

SXSW allowed the company the perfect venue to both test elastic demand in a real world setting and capture the attention of the tech press. Approximately 30,000 registered attendees came to Austin for the conference, many bringing family with them, while additional thousands flocked to the film and music portion of the festival. All of those people needed to get around and SideCar offered them both transportation and the coveted "gee whiz" experience.

Sidecar uses a smartphone app to match everyday drivers with clients in need of a ride. The fees are shared by the driver and Sidecar. Costs average 10% less than comparable taxi fares with a much higher perceived sense of availability, reliability, and safety. In San Francisco, the company found that its heaviest repeat customers were 20-something women.

Like any company with a solid growth strategy, SideCar tests its data in the cities where it launches. Currently the service is available in San Francisco, Seattle, Los Angeles, Philadelphia, Austin, Boston, Brooklyn, Washington D.C., Charlotte, Chicago, San Diego, Long Beach, and Oakland.

In an attempt to understand and achieve market fit, Sidecar is catering to a marked decline in car ownership among 20-somethings. For this age group, driving presents problems at multiple levels, starting with the "don't text and drive" conundrum.

The 18-24 age bracket of smartphone owners sends and receives more than 4,000 text messages per month, a decidedly unsafe and typically illegal activity behind the wheel. The traditional idea has been that car ownership equates with freedom.

For this age group, however, real freedom is simply having ready access to transportation that meets their needs. The fact that Sidecar is smartphone based further caters to this ethos since the basic assumption is that the smartphone is the central hub of activity and means of organization and connection for the current crop of twenty-somethings.

Within this age bracket, the sharing economy has gained considerable traction as evidence by the success of other startups with a similar philosophical bent like AirBnB. With services like Sidecar, all parties benefit — riders and drivers.

The latest iteration of the Sidecar app lets user tailor their rides by type of vehicle type, driver, and price as well as proximity to their current location. As proof of the traction of the sharing concept, during its first summer in operation, Sidecar snapped up an addition $10 million in funding.

Sidecar also stays focused on the user experience. People who have taken rides with Sidecar drivers said they felt they were being driven by a friend — to the point that they weren't upset about missed turns or other benign "mistakes."

They sat up front, had a nice chat with the driver, and left the car smiling. That kind of goodwill generates the Holy Grail of growth hacking, word of mouth from satisfied customers.

Mashable

In 2005, then 19-year-old Pete Cashmore founded Mashable from his home in Aberdeen, Scotland because he wanted to do something productive — from bed. In its earliest iteration the site was a blog that focused on social media news.

Four years later, Time magazine named Mashable among the 25 best blogs for 2009 and it had become a destination point for readers seeking tech coverage. Initially, Cashmore did nothing more than try to find compelling content, most of it regurgitated from other sources, re-cast the material in a tone his core audience would enjoy, and hopefully pay for it all with Google ads.

He closed his first real ad deal in 2006. That brought in a few thousand dollars a month, which he used to hire a small staff. His philosophy has been one of doing as much as possible with very few resources and always re-investing in his product. Along the way, he also legitimized the idea of blogging as a business.

In multiple interviews over the years, Cashmore has described his position on keeping Mashable what he calls "consumer facing." User experience is everything as that relates to reporting and curation that puts interesting and potentially useful material in front of the reader — again, the concept of market fit.

–
As other sites like Quora have found out, in spite of the text-intensive nature of the web, users don't necessarily like

to read, and they are often overwhelmed by the sheer volume of potential content. Mashable's focus is on curating or aggregating stories of interest to their audience, thus acting as both a filter and a timesaver. The payoff is both user engagement and brand loyalty.

By 2009, Mashable boasted 5 million visits per month, a number that grew to 12.5 million by 2012. In 2013, Cashmore declined to sell the site to CNN, announcing in January 2014 that his company had raised $13.3 million in an equity investment, the first time Mashable has taken on outside investors.

The money will be used to fuel Mashable's one consistent growth engine — content. The site continues to derive its revenue from advertising, and has been a leader in the emerging field of branded or native content, which is ads that look like news.

In some cases the material will carry a tagline reading "sponsored by" or "presented by" the advertising corporation. In others, Mashable is paid to write material on a given theme with the company's ads running alongside the story. Since the site now attracts 30 million unique visitors around the globe each month, the potential reach of that kind of marketing is highly attractive to companies.

The common thread in all of Mashable's content is speaking to the millennial generation and people who think like them. The site now covers tech, business, social media, entertainment, and a host of other topics from a web-savvy perspective.

In many ways the Mashable story is very old-fashioned, one-man-with-a-vision tale, while in another, it is an example of single-minded understanding of market focus with inherent flexibility to shift with the prevailing interest. Regardless, the growth has been impressive and highly effective.

99designs

The online graphics design marketplace 99designs was founded in Melbourne, Australia in 2008 to create products via crowdsourcing. Designs are entered competitively for customer selection in a contest structure with the winner receiving cash payment. There is also an option to purchase templates and work with individual designers directly. Typical projects include logos, t-shirts, and websites.

Traction for solid growth was actually built in to the concept from the beginning since it was a spinoff of SitePoint forums. Participating web designers on the forums occasionally competed informally in fictional logo contests. Ultimately someone asked for the real thing and the idea was born to spin off a company.

99designs was profitable from year one because they began with proof of concept and then achieved fast internationalization by bootstrapping their existing U.S.-based traffic through the forums. The company opened in the United States in 2010 and secured $35 million in funding the following year. In 2012, after acquiring 12designer, 99designs entered the European market.

The spin-off story is a good example of how growth hacking should follow inspiration and user demand. It would have been easy to blow off the request for a real-life logo contest as a flash in the pan, but the 99design organizers saw merit in the competition model.

From the start, they understood the demands of market fit. This was behind their decision to keep their development team in Australia even when U.S. customers represented their largest market, and to remain localized to English-language jobs for the first three years.

During that period, the company still worked with customers in 150 countries, but they were able to learn more about the markets they hoped to enter and to add to their existing pool of designers.

When 99designs did enter the European market, they did so with the acquisition of an existing firm (12designer) that was already localized in five languages. At the time, 99designs was well capitalized and could afford to stretch their marketing budget.

By 2012, the site's top designers were making upwards of $10,000 a month. In January 2012 alone, the entire 99design community earned a total $1.5 million. At that point, four years into its existence, the company paid out $28 million to its designers, who work on a commission model, earning anywhere from 30%-50% of the purchase price for their work.

Tumblr

The microblogging platform Tumblr debuted in February 2007, a year after its main competitor, Twitter was launched. At this juncture of the blogging phenomenon, many people wanted to maintain a blog but couldn't commit to writing long, interesting posts.

For those for whom Twitter's constantly rolling 140 character updates did not form a coherent narrative, Tumblr seemed a perfect answer. The service allowed for simple short-form multi-media posting from a dashboard interface and some degree of social networking with users following one another.

Within two weeks, the site gained 75,000 users simply because it filled a desire on the part of frustrated would-be bloggers (and some existing bloggers) who wanted a shorter, faster option. Since the founder, David Karp, was a software engineer, he was able to design an excellent and simple user experience from Tumblr's inception that gained rapid traction.

In May 2013, Yahoo! bought Tumblr for approximately $1.1 billion and today the site plays host to more than 184 million blogs. Little has changed in the intervening period since, in one of those rare moments of serendipity, Tumblr achieved market fit from day one.

Tumblr currently derives revenue from selling themes and allowing its users to have "sponsored" posts. In testament to the ongoing popularity of this middle ground blogging solution, Tumblr manages to retain more than 85% of its sign-ups, with Twitter keeping only 30%.

Like other services, however, the Tumblr mobile app has seen significant improvement, with the ability to customize the user's profile, raising the potential for the site to see a second revitalization in connected devices. The simplistic Tumblr model is perfect for mobile users, where blogging has always been unnecessarily difficult.

Seen in this way, Tumblr might be able to carve out a more unique identity for itself if it can strike the sweet spot between Instagram's photo intensive ecosphere and Facebook's tendency to overshare. Tumblr offers users more control over appearance and content copy on the go that may well have more relevancy for millenials.

In mid-2014, the release of the updated and more powerful app led 80% of active users to re-customize their blogs, which points to a powerful resurgence in interest. This is refinement in the best tradition of growth hacking and makes Tumblr a company to watch for a new levels of expansion.

Ingenious Growth Hacks

While each of these companies offer excellent examples of growth hacking in action, everyone seems to want to arrive at the "top" growth hacks of all time list. I've already talked about the AirBnB hack to integrate under the radar with Craigslist, but here's a compilation (in no particular order) of some of the tactics that always seem to make the cut:

- Hotmail really is considered one of the classics of growth hacking, and it was a simplistic and ingenious move. That tag line at the bottom of every email, "Get your free email at Hotmail," took the service from 3000 users to 1 million in 6 months. That one probably will always hold first place on any list because it was and is brilliant.

- The Facebook option to tag someone in a photo sends an email to that person, an action that generates almost a 75% click through rate to the site. The emotional pull is almost irresistible. What's the picture? What did they say? Is my Mother going to see that? In a true culture of growth, Facebook still has a growth team, even though it's the largest social network in the world.

- The Dropbox option to invite a friend and get 500mb of storage kicks up the user's social reaction and self-interest. Once a Dropbox user really understands what the service can do for them, especially in storing and sharing large photo files, the desire for more space at no cost is almost automatic.

- Pinterest applies an incredibly simple way to remove any perceived friction from their browsing experience – the ultimate scroll. You can go to Pinterest and look, and look, and look, and look and never click once. Are people really that lazy? Absolutely, but at the same time, this technique creates stickiness and ultimately will draw them deeper and deeper into the site.

- Instagram does something similar with their feed via their mobile app. To speed load time, they put only the most popular photos first, which encourages scrolling and encourages users to add and share their own photos. Both Pinterest and Instagram are heavily dependent on the power of visual appeal and have optimized their feeds brilliantly to capitalize on that experience.

- There are some pretty brilliant game-based growth hacks out there as well. In mid-2013, the game Candy Crush was reporting 45 million users per month. How? By its very design Candy Crush creates sweet tooth addicts. When a user "dies," they either have to wait 30 minutes for a timer reset, pay for more lives to play again, or go out begging / inviting friends to sign up and help them out.

Learning to Growth Hack

It's important to understand from the beginning that there is no *one* way to achieve company growth. In fact, the very nature of growth hacking pushes against complacency and formulaic approaches.

No growth hacker should ever see their role in a company as static, nor should they look for growth that follows a single curve.

Truly effective growth is both steady *and* rapid. The best curve to grow a business looks more like a jagged set of steps going up the side of a mountain than a smooth curve. Think about that image for a minute.

- Periods of slow, steady growth allow for testing, development, and strategic planning.

- Periods of rapid, unsustainable growth achieve new plateaus, infuse the endeavor with energy, and if well analyzed, suggest new directions.

Merged into one upward pattern, these two types of growth represent true and building momentum.

Art, Not Science

Remember, growth hacking is more art than science and demands that the growth hacker have the ability to constantly adapt to an organization's changing needs. People who like routine or who are wedded to doing things one way for long periods of time don't make good growth hackers!

Always ask yourself:

- What does the customer or the market want?

- Who are my customers / users?

- Where do I find my customers / users?

- What language do my customers / users speak?

It's a wise course of action to do NOTHING until you know your market. Just look at Goodreads and Amazon.

Goodreads was founded by a voracious reader who also happened to be a coder. Amazon was founded by an entrepreneur who looked at what could be sold online and settled on books due to historic demand and the passionate attachment of readers to literature.

It's worth noting that Jeff Bezos ruled out video, audio, and computers as the basis for the Amazon store, but then came back when he had the capital and incorporated those items and many more into the now giant retail site.

His reason for the gradual expansion was incredibly sound. People who buy books also tend to buy music and videos. He then merged those interests into a neat consumer electronics package with the Kindle Fire tablet, an all-in-one device for consuming Amazon content — ebooks, music, and video with built-in on-the-device ordering. Now THAT'S knowing your market.

It didn't happen all at once, but Bezos understood the desires of his customers and has continued to innovate in a direction that meets their growing and changing tastes. Oh. And along the way, he bought Goodreads, the largest online social community for readers and completely integrated its use in the Kindle line of ebook readers. Genius.

A Growth Oriented Company Culture

It's good wisdom to follow the dictate that the concept of growth has to be hardwired into a business or product from day one — as the example of Jeff Bezos clearly illustrates.

Ideally, this attitude should be cultivated by the founder of the endeavor as the one who sets the tone for a growth "creed" and directs the allocation of resources to realize that vision. Typically the realization happens along the lines of the curve I described in the opening of this chapter, sharp growth spikes punctuated with plateaus for measurement and reassessment.

In a best-case-scenario the founder of a company is also the endeavor's first and chief growth hacker, even though he is likely to pass that responsibility on to others once the business is out of the start-up phase.

People who successfully grow businesses tend to be generalists, a trait often seen in successful entrepreneurs —

and they should also have vision. That translates to good intuition for product, and an ability to fill multiple roles while keeping their eyes on the ultimate goal.

All Growth Hackers Aren't Coders

It's a mistake, however, to assume that all growth hackers also have to be coders. Certainly it's an ideal situation if you have someone who is both a software engineer and a brilliant, innovative marketer with a sense of product-market fit.

Those people are, however, about as common as mythical unicorns. If you can articulate your needs and explain how you perceive gaining initial traction, software engineers can be hired to make it happen.

The same results can be achieved by either party, it's simply a matter of how the questions are posed to trigger the development of solutions.

- A growth hacker who is a coder might look at an aspect of the user experience and think, "There has to be a way to automate that."

- A growth hacker who isn't a coder is the guy who walks into the software engineer's office and says, "Do you think you can find a way to automate that?"

The two types can be very powerful partners since coders tend to become growth hackers the longer they are a part of a growth hacking team. By nature their minds are analytical and trend toward problem solving.

Most programmers have, at one time or another, chafed under the constraints of the limited imagination of management. Growth hacking is about testing, measuring, and trying out new concepts.

Creative people thrive in that environment and although they may not consider themselves growth hackers in the beginning, they are often the very ones to say, "Hey, what would happen if . . . ?"

When the person listening to creative ideas that fall outside of the proverbial box is open and receptive to innovation, the whole team effort becomes supercharged.

The take away from these observations is to develop a sound concept and never stop working to find and hone market fit. Hire the best people you can find. Share your vision. Make sure they understand it. And then work the data over and over again.

Replicable Strategies are Golden

Any strategy that can be used repeatedly and gets better with each iteration is golden. Companies like Uber are a good example. They perfected a city-wide roll out strategy in San Francisco that proved to be so effective they have used and improved it in each successive city they enter.

Even in the face of replicable success, however, the focus should remain on delivering the best user / customer experience, even if that means completely changing the direction of the endeavor midstream. RelayRides is a good example of an incredibly successful change in course.

They started out believing that their ride sharing concept was best targeted for short-term hourly hires and wound up completely focusing their business on long-term rentals with airport based drop off and pick up. Why?

The company introduced its service at San Francisco International Airport where it was so well received, the concept was then implemented in 229 additional airports. In short order, RelayRides was gaining 95% of their revenue from a long-term hiring model and discontinued hourly rentals.

A replicable growth hacking strategy for a company might look something like this:

- Figure out what data to track that will give you the greatest insight into your user base and its behavior.

- Perform the necessary analytics to understand that behavior and extract the maximum benefit and insight from it.

- Prioritize the actions that will most facilitate growth and do those first, even if re-design or the inclusion of new features and/or directions is required.

- Build and push changes as reflected under prioritization. Measure again and gauge your success.

Obviously these steps are customized per product and business model, but you get the idea. Test, refine, implement — over, and over, and over again.

Markets Are Always in Flux

Never fall into the trap of assuming you have achieved perfect market fit. Markets are constantly in flux. What you do to gain traction in a market may not be the answer to sustaining and growing your user base. Almost all of the truly great growth hacks are, at the base level, answers to optimization problems.

- The Hotmail tagline was a simple and elegant refinement to every email message sent through the service that made each email a marketing tool.

- The AirBnB hack neatly cross-posted listings to Craigslist, bootstrapping the booking service's user base off the existing Craiglist ecosystem.

- The Pinterest invite-only beta successfully generated interest and seeded the site with high quality pins from professional designers.

Each of these growth hacks and less flashy techniques like Twitter's suggested followers, Instagram's cross-posting options, and Dropox's incentivized referrals are all examples of optimizing presentation and enhancing the user experience.

There is no such thing as "good enough" in growth hacking, where even shaving a few seconds off a site's load time can have value if it answers a clearly identified user need or removes a potential point of friction.

Scrappy, even black hat, techniques like AirBnB's hack of Craigslist may be responsible for first stage growth, but the problems generally get more complicated when retention, monetization, and acquisition enter the equation.

Lots of start-ups take off like a rocket only to fizzle for lack of sustained growth. Always maintain the attitude that something you are doing can be done better.

"Do or Do Not, There is No Try"

Okay, yeah, I blatantly lifted that from Yoda, but in the end result the way to learn to growth hack is to growth hack — not to try it, but just to *do* it. One of the most attractive aspects of this philosophy of marketing is that mistakes aren't just "allowed," but are a *good thing* because they are taken as opportunities from which people just move on.

"Do overs" are encouraged and changing your mind is a virtue, but ONLY when done in the name of achieving the ultimate goal of growth and ONLY in response to measurable data reflecting user behavior and articulated needs. This is the matter of "product / market fit" and it's EVERYTHING.

While you're working your own growth hacking strategies, immerse yourself in what other growth hackers are doing. Read case studies like those I have included in this text. Get ideas from idea people. The specific growth hack may not apply to your product or your business model, but it might inspire you to do something similar — or even NOT to do something.

Growth Hacking Reference Sources

There are a plethora of online resources on growth hacking to broaden your understanding and learn from the "masters." Here are some of my favorites to get you started:

- "What is 'Growth Hacking' Really?" by Josh Elan at medium.com/what-i-learned-building/f445b04cbd20

- "Defining A Growth Hacker: Three Common Characteristics" at techcrunch.com/2012/09/02/defining-a-growth-hacker-three-common-characteristics/

- "The Definitive Guide to Growth Hacking" at www.quicksprout.com/2013/08/26/the-definitive-guide-to-growth-hacking/

- "Defining A Growth Hacker: Debunking The 6 Most Common Myths About Growth Hacking" at techcrunch.com/2012/12/08/defining-a-growth-hacker-6-myths-about-growth-hackers/

- "Defining A Growth Hacker: Building Growth into Your Team" at techcrunch.com/2012/10/21/defining-a-growth-hacker-building-growth-into-your-team/

- "How to Hire a Growth Hacker" at www.aginnt.com/post/64205739421/how-to-hire-a-growth-hacker#.U2_ZiK1dXR1

- "13 Critically Important Lessons from Over 50 Growth Hackers" at blog.kissmetrics.com/lessons-from-growth-hackers/

- "What is a Growth Hacker? Does Your Startup Need a Growth Team?" at www.caneelian.com/2012/10/30/what-is-a-growth-hacker-does-your-startup-need-a-growth-team/

Like all things online, these links can go away thanks to the changing nature of the web, but the links were all good at the time of this writing in mid-2014.

Growth Hacking Itself Will Evolve

Growth hacking is itself an evolving and changing field. Even the definition of what it means to "grow" is changing in the face of the growing mobile revolution.

Experts predict that by the end of 2014, there will be 90 million tablet computer users in the United States alone. Some of these people may lead their entire online lives without ever sitting down at a conventional desktop PC or opening a laptop.

Knowing this, optimizing a user experience for the tablet generation will be much different than tailoring a site to meet the needs of a PC user. A good growth hacker doesn't just stay on top of trends of this nature, but anticipates them and factors them into their ongoing strategy.

That is both the daunting and exciting aspect of this new approach to marketing in the 21st century. It's no longer a matter of thinking outside the box, but of redesigning the box, or even asking, "Why do we have a box in the first place?"

Afterword

While I was researching material for this book, I ran across a Slideshare presentation by Ryan Holiday entitled "19 Growth Hacker Quotes: Thoughts on the Future of Marketing" that seem to further support the notion I raised in the foreword that defining growth hacking is like nailing Jell-o to a tree.

- Growth hackers have a common attitude, internal investigation process, and mentality unique among technologist and marketers. This mindset of data, creativity, and curiosity allows a growth hacker to accomplish the feat of grown a user base into the millions. — Andrew Chen, Entrepreneur and Technology Writer

- A growth hacker works within the parameters of a scalable and repeatable method for growth, drive by product and inspired by data. A growth hacker lives at the intersection of data, product, and marketing. — Aaron Ginn, Head of Grown, StumbleUpon

- Growth hacking has a subtle message of "what have you done for me today?" You never stop as a growth hacker. Facebook still has a growth team and they have a billion users. - Blake Commagere, Founder of MediaSpike

- "Growth hacking" is a recognition that when you focus on understanding your users and how they discover and adopt your products, you can build features that help you acquire and retain more users, rather than just spending marketing dollars. — Josh Elman, Partner at Greylock Partners

- Growth hacking is the process and mindset of searching for k ways that your product to grow. It's kind of like a mix between engineering and marketing. The key is to find untapped channels of customers that are motivated to use your product. — Dan Martell, Founder of Clarity

- A growth hacker is someone who has thrown out the playbook of traditional marketing and replaced it with only what is testable, trackable, and scalable. Their tools are emails, pay-per-click ads, blogs, and platform APIs instead of commercials, publicity, and money.

- Growth hacking tends to be more "experience" focused. This includes driving engagement and sharing within a product or spreading a product experience across networks. Effective growth hackers are relentless about running creative experiments and optimizing the components of the experiment until finding something that works. - Sean Ellis, CEO of Qualaroo

Perhaps my favorite however is by David Ogilvy, known as "the father of advertising." It speaks to both the serious detail orientation of growth hacking and the relentless curiosity and urge to optimize that goes with it:

- "I prefer the discipline of knowledge to the anarchy of ignorance. We pursue knowledge the way a pig pursues truffles."

Growth hackers are all these things — and whatever else they need to be in the situation in which they find themselves. They are self-inventors in many ways, and re-inventors of most of the things with which they come into contact.

That is, frankly, one of the most intriguing things about this way to market, the complete absence of "rules," but an ever expanding playbook. If a growth hacker throws a Hail Mary pass, you can bet that he knows the prevailing wind speed, weight of the ball, and potential reach of the receiver in the end zone down to the millimeter.

Now, if there's two seconds left on the clock and he can get away with rigging the danged thing to hang up until that ball is caught and the ref's arms are up in the air? He'll do that, too.

Relevant Books, and Articles

http://www.GrowthHacking.Me – Receive FREE Growth hacking videos and latest news.

Blaut, Jacek. "21 User Acquisition Growth Hacks You Need to Know." growthhackingpro.com/21-user-acquisition-growth-hacks/

Casanova, Jose. *Growth Hacking: A How To Guide on Becoming a Growth Hacker.* White Owl Publishing, 2013.

Chen, Andrew. *The Viral Startup: A Guide to Designing Viral Loops.* Hyperlink, 2013.

Croll, Alistair. *Lean Analytics: Use Data to Build a Better Startup Faster.* O'Reilly, 2013.

Ellis, Sean. *Lean Marketing for Startups: Agile Product Development, Business Model Design, Web Analytics, and Other Keys to Rapid Growth.* (See www.startup-marketing.com)

Ginn, Aaron. "Defining a Growth Hacker: Three Common Characteristics." techcrunch.com/2012/09/02/defining-a-growth-hacker-three-common-characteristics/

Holiday, Ryan. *Growth Hacker Marketing: A Primer on the Future PR, Marketing, and Advertising.* Portfolio, 2013.

Maurya, Ash. *Running Lean: Iterate from Plan A to a Plan That Works.* O'Reilly Media, 2012.

McClure, Dave. "Startup Metrics 4 Pirates." Slideshare presentation at www.slideshare.net/dmc500hats/startup-metrics-for-pirates-nov-2012

Ries, Eric. *The Lean Startup: How Today's entrepreneurs Use Continuous Innovation to Create Radically Successful Businesses.* Crown Business, 2011.

Schranz, Thomas. *Growth Engineering 101: A Step-by-Step Guide for Founders, Product Managers and Marketers.* (See www.blossom.io/growth-engineering)

Vilner, Yoav. "Growth Jacking 101: Read This to Become a Magician." www.ranky.co/growth-hacking-101-read-become-magician/

Yongfook, Jon. "21 Actionable Growth Hacking Tactics." yongfook.com/actionable-growth-hacking-tactics.html

Marketing Terminology Used in Growth Hacking

The more you read about growth hacking, there are many marketing terms you will encounter. While this is not a definitive glossary, these are some of the terms you may encounter in the growth hacking book:

A/B Testing

A/B Testing refers to the comparison of two variables or versions to identify the best performer to use in support of a growth or optimization goal. This might include, but is not limited to: versions of emails, variations in calls to action like buttons or links, and the arrangement of elements on a landing page.

Analytics

Analytics are mechanisms for looking at patterns of data in how websites are accessed and utilized. This might include number of visitors, time on the site, links clicked, and so forth.

API

API stands for "application programming interface" and is the means by which software components are allowed to interact with one another.

Brand

When used as a noun, a brand refers to anything (product, service, or corporate identity) that distinguishes one product from another, which can be the design or name of the thing, or a symbol, design, or logo associated with it. When used as a verb, "branding" the term refers to the creation of such a distinct identification.

Call-to-Action

Anything on a site that elicits a response from a user that initiates an action, preferably contact, subscriptions, or membership, is called a "call to action." This might be an image, button, or text link.

Content

Any piece of information that has been produced to be digested by visitors that is informative, engaging, and hopefully elicits sharing as a result is referred to as content. This can be anything from an article or blog post to a video, slideshow, or podcast.

Landing Page

A website's landing page is the first page (also called the home page) that is visible when someone reaches the site either by clicking an inbound link or typing the site's address into a browser.

Metric

As it relates to marketing and growth hacking, a metric is any system or standard of measurement particularly that used to quantify an aspect of performance for a business or product.

Pay-Per-Click

The pay-per-click business model is one in which an advertising or member business on a site is charged only when a user actually clicks on their link to initiate an action or purchase.

Product/Market Fit

Product/Market fit is the delivery of a product or serve that perfectly satisfies the need of a given user segment and thus creates a loyal and passionate user base.

SEO (Search Engine Optimization)

Search engine optimizations are augmentations or enhancement to websites that ensure that the page is as visible as possible to search engines and thus will appear at the top of a results page.

SEM (Search Engine Marketing)

Any marketing practice that is geared toward improving a site's search engine visibility included search engine optimization or paying or placement on a search engine results page.

Social Commerce

The term social commerce describes online retail and marketing strategies that incorporate established social networks and peer-to-peer communications as a driver of sales.

Virality

Any piece of information online, whether it is an article, image, or video, that is widely shared and circulates rapidly is said to have "gone viral" and thus possesses "virality."

Index

Suggestions / Reviews

I really hope you liked the book and found it useful.

Please would you be kind enough to leave me a review.

A LOT of time and hard work went into writing it and I would be very grateful if you could leave a review please.

I hope you found some ideas to inspire you. How can you change the techniques featured in this book and apply it to your business?

If you are unhappy with the book or feel I have missed information out then please do get in contact and hopefully I can help.
I'm happy to rewrite / add sections if you feel it would improve the book for other readers in the future. Simply email me (unfortunately the publishers would not allow me to use my personal email address but they have promised to forward every email on. So please contact me at growthhacking@bleppublishing.com with your suggestions.

I'll get back to you as soon as I can (it may take a few days) If I can I will then act on your ideas and revise the book and send you a free copy (and others who joined our free club via http://www.growthhacking.me) with the updated book ASAP just as a 'thank you' for helping to improve it.
Thank you again
Robert Peters